WORKING SPACES
ESPACES DE TRAVAIL
RAUM FÜR ARBEIT

WORKING SPACES
ESPACES DE TRAVAIL
RAUM FÜR ARBEIT

EVERGREEN

EVERGREEN is an imprint of

Taschen GmbH

© 2005 TASCHEN GmbH

Hohenzollernring 53, D-50672 Köln

www.taschen.com

Editor Editrice Redakteur:
Simone Schleifer

French translation Traduction française Französische Übersetzung:
Marion Westerhoff

German translation Traduction allemande Deutsche Übersetzung:
Grusche Rosenkranz

English proof reading Relecture anglaise Korrektur lesen:
Matthew Clarke

Art director Direction artistique Art Direktor:
Mireia Casanovas Soley

Graphic design and layout Mise en page et maquette Graphische Gestaltung und Layout:
Diego González

Printed by Imprimé en Gedruckt durch:
Anman Gràfiques del Vallès, Spain

ISBN: 3-8228-4186-2

Contents Index Inhalt

The rapid development of new kinds of lifestyles over the past 20th century has given rise to a new philosophy of work and new ways of carrying out professional activities. The idea of transforming the working area into an integrated part of the domestic space is now a familiar concept, and freelance professionals often opt to establish their office at home not only for financial reasons but also for the opportunity to work within a personalized space that is both attractive and comfortable. More and more professionals are finding themselves confronted with unusual spaces that need to be adapted to the evolving living and working habits of modern society.

Since the beginning of the twentieth century, when bohemian artists started living out of their studios, people of all professions have been incorporating their working space into the home. In the case of artists, it was mostly a matter of physical and economic convenience; they were free to act on their inspiration at any given moment while also reducing their housing expenses.

Nowadays, there are many other reasons for working from home. As cities have grown larger, so have the distances between office and home, making commuting more arduous and less appealing. Furthermore, the strict eight-hour working day has become less commonplace and many professionals pursue alternative careers in the evenings. Even more crucial, however, is the advent of information technology, which offers the possibility of exchanging information in seconds by merely typing on a keyboard.

The concept of freelance work was born and, since then, countless professionals have established their offices in their lofts, houses, and apartments, with practical and attractive results that vary in shape, size, and style. While some prefer to physically separate office and home into two separate entities, others use enclosures, partitions, and variations in level to comfortably fit both functions under the same roof, or, by choice or through lack of physical space, combine their work and home within a single area, dissolving the boundaries between the two.

This book has gathered 69 projects from around the world that represent the latest trends in working space design; each project is the work of a contemporary architect, interior designer, or homeowner who has used striking and ingenious ideas to create a distinctive working area. This book offers a multitude of ideas for anyone interested in creating their own home-studio.

Au cours du XXe siècle, l'essor rapide de styles de vie différents a engendré une nouvelle philosophie du travail et d'autres modes d'exercice de l'activité professionnelle. L'idée d'intégrer l'aire de travail à l'espace privé est devenue monnaie courante. Les personnes, qui travaillent en free-lance, optent souvent pour cette solution. Ceci, non seulement pour des raisons financières mais souvent pour travailler dans le confort d'un cadre personnalisé, agréable. De ce fait, de plus en plus de professionnels doivent adapter des espaces inhabituels aux nouveaux modes de vie et de travail de la société actuelle.

Dès les prémices du XXe siècle, les artistes bohèmes ont commencé à vivre dans leurs ateliers. Depuis, les gens exerçant d'autres métiers, intègrent aussi leur local professionnel à leur domicile. Dans le cas des artistes, c'était surtout pour des raisons financières et de convenance personnelle. Ils pouvaient ainsi, à tout moment, travailler au gré de leur inspiration, et ceci à moindres frais.

De nos jours, d'autres arguments se sont greffés en faveur du travail à domicile. Avec l'expansion des villes, les distances entre domicile et bureau se sont accentuées, rendant le trajet quotidien de plus en plus fastidieux. En outre, devant la réduction du temps de travail - le régime strict de huit heures quotidiennes s'étant assoupli - de nombreuses personnes exercent, le soir, d'autres activités professionnelles. Mais le tournant décisif est marqué par l'avènement de l'informatique et la possibilité d'échanger des informations en quelques secondes, avec dans leur sillage, la recrudescence du travail en free-lance. D'innombrables professionnels installent leur bureau à domicile dans leur loft, maison ou appartement : créations d'espaces conjuguant esthétisme et commodité, dans un éventail varié de formes, de tailles et de styles. Là, où certains préfèrent une séparation physique entre bureau et domicile, créant deux entités, d'autres adoptent annexes, cloisons et différences de niveaux pour accueillir les deux fonctions sous le même toit. Enfin, d'aucuns, par choix délibéré ou par manque de place, réunissent travail et domicile en un seul espace, dans un décloisonnement total.

Cet ouvrage réunit 69 projets phare, témoins des dernières tendances du design d'espaces professionnels, à l'échelle mondiale. Chaque projet est l'œuvre d'un architecte contemporain, d'un designer d'intérieur ou d'un propriétaire qui a développé des idées ingénieuses, intéressantes pour créer une aire de travail originale. Ce livre offre une multitude d'idées à tous ceux qui désirent créer leur bureau à domicile.

Im letzten Jahrhundert hat die schnelle Entwicklung neuer Arten von Lifestyle eine neue Arbeits-ethik sowie neue Modelle und berufliche Aktivitäten hervorgerufen. Die Idee, den Arbeitsbereich zu einem integrierten Teil im Wohnbereich zu machen, ist heute ein geläufiges Konzept und Selbst-ständige entscheiden sich oft nicht nur aus finanziellen Gründen dafür, ihr Büro Zuhause zu instal-lieren, sondern genießen auch das Gefühl, in einem persönlichen Bereich zu arbeiten, den sie nach ihren eigenen Vorstellungen geschaffen haben. Immer mehr Arbeiter werden dabei mit ungewöhn-lichen Räumen konfrontiert, die angepasst werden müssen an die sich entwickelnden Lebens- und Arbeitsgewohnheiten der modernen Gesellschaft.

Seit Beginn des 20. Jh., als die Künstler der Boheme mit ihren Studios ein Vorbild schufen, haben Menschen aller Berufssparten den Arbeitsplatz zu sich nach Hause verlegt. Im Falle der Künstler war es oft eine physische und wirtschaftliche Notwendigkeit. Sie konnten so jederzeit ihrer Inspi-ration freien Lauf lassen und gleichzeitig die Wohnraumkosten niedrig halten.

Heute gibt es noch viele weitere Gründe, um von Zuhause aus zu arbeiten. Die Städte sind grö-ßer geworden, die Entfernung zwischen Wohn- und Arbeitsplatz ebenfalls, pendeln wird immer beschwerlicher und verliert an Attraktivität. Den strikten Achtstundentag gibt es heute häufig nicht mehr und viele Menschen arbeiten auch in den Abendstunden an einer zweiten Karriere. Noch wichtiger aber ist der Einfluss der Informationstechnologie, die den Austausch von Information innerhalb von Sekunden ermöglicht.

Das Konzept der selbstständigen Arbeit war geboren und seitdem haben viele Menschen ihren Berufsalltag in ihre Dachböden, Häuser und Wohnungen verlagert, was durchaus zu praktischen und attraktiven Ergebnissen in Bezug auf Größe, Form und Stil führte. Während manch einer Büro und Haushalt gern trennt, nisten sich andere in einem Erker, hinter einer Trennwand oder einer Reihe anderer Nischen ein, um beide Funktionen unter einem Dach zu vereinen. Wo der Raum keine Trennung vorgibt, werden Arbeit und Freizeit auch in einem Bereich miteinander vereint und die Grenzen gehen fließend ineinander über.

In diesem Buch wurden 69 Projekte aus der ganzen Welt zusammengestellt, die den neuesten Trend im Design von Arbeitsbereichen repräsentieren. Jedes einzelne Projekt entwarfen moderne Architekten, Innenarchitekten oder Hausbesitzer. Dabei sind außergewöhnliche und raffinierte Ideen umgesetzt worden, die einen ganz eigenen Arbeitsbereich schaffen. Dieses Buch bietet jedem, der sein eigenes Home-Office einrichten möchte, eine Reihe von interessanten Ansätzen.

Barcelona, Spain

Cloud 9

One of the main reasons of the team members was to show that the new space had the young and creative character of the company. Previously this space was a carpenter's workshop. It had an attic which was supported by a wall that crossed the whole shop and an interior patio. The studio had hidden qualities and potentials, so the decision was made to do away with the attic and make maximum use of the size of the space. After the wall that led to the patio was taken down, it was replaced with glass so as to gain more light. One single piece of furniture was installed, which is the crux for understanding: the computer network, the main table, the bookcase, the filing cabinet, and the storage space. The work areas are identical and unchangeable. This piece of furniture is where work is done, where meetings are held; facilitated by rotating chairs, the common room and a place of interactions.

L'une des motivations majeures des intégrants de cet équipe était de trouver un nouvel espace correspondant au caractère jeune et innovant de la compagnie. Cet espace abritait auparavant un atelier de menuiserie qui disposait d'un grenier soutenu par un mur traversant tout le magasin et un patio intérieur. Le studio offrant des possibilités cachées, il fut décidé de supprimer l'attique afin de tirer parti au maximum du volume de l'espace. Le mur conduisant au patio a été supprimé et remplacé par une cloison de verre laissant pénétrer davantage de lumière. Un seul meuble polyvalent a été installé, clé de voûte de la conception : réseau d'ordinateurs, table principale, bibliothèque, meuble de classement des dossiers et espace de rangement. Les aires de bureau sont identiques et fixes. Ce meuble est l'endroit où se fait le travail et où se tiennent les réunions. Il est agrémenté de chaises pivotantes, d'une pièce commune et d'un espace polyvalent.

Einer der Hauptgründe für den Umzug des Büros von Cloud 9 war es, den jungen und kreativen Charakter des Unternehmens mehr in den Vordergrund zu rücken. Dieser Raum war vorher die Werkstatt eines Tischlers. Es gehörten dazu ein Dachboden, der von einer Wand gehalten wurde, die durch die gesamte Werkstatt reichte und ein Innenhof hinter einer weiteren Wand. Man entschied, den Dachboden zu entfernen. Danach wurde auch die Wand zum Hof durch eine Glaswand ersetzt, um mehr natürliches Tageslicht eindringen zu lassen. Ein einziges Möbelstück wurde installiert, welches alle anderen integriert hat: das Computernetzwerk, den Haupttisch, das Regal, die Ablage und den Laderaum. Die Arbeitsbereiche sind identisch und fest verankert. Hier werden neben der Arbeit auch Meetings abgehalten.

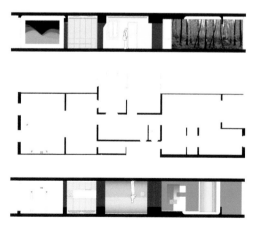

› Plan Plan Grundriss

In order to create colorful reflections on the surfaces, the floor was painted pistachio green and the furniture treated with white lacquer.

Pour que les surfaces renvoient les reflets de couleurs et de lumière, le sol a été peint couleur vert pistache et le mobilier recouvert de laque.

Um Farbreflexe auf den Oberflächen zu erzeugen, wurde der Boden Pistaziengrün gestrichen und die Möbel mit weißem Lack angemalt.

Dwelling for an executive
Maison pour un directeur
Haus für eine Geschäftsfrau

São Paulo, Brazil

This apartment combines some earlier elements and all the features of the architect's work: nerve, light, color, modernity, aestheticism and investigation in terms of the materials and the possibilities of the space. The element that stands out in the apartment is the colored glass, which helps to create enveloping and seductive atmospheres, and brings a feeling of spaciousness to the place. Fraccaroli has opted for a versatile structure that separates the living room and bedroom with a panel of green glass. In this way, the separation of the two environments comes from different points of light, all of which redesign the space on their own. This effect empowers the usefulness of the apartment and matches with the needs of its inhabitant, who is looking for efficiency and convenience in an elegant environment and with a certain luxury that goes with her profession.

Cet appartement conjugue éléments anciens et toutes les caractéristiques de l'œuvre de l'architecte : dynamisme, lumière, couleur, modernisme, esthétique et recherche au niveau des matériaux et de l'espace. Le verre coloré est l'élément mis en relief dans cet appartement. Il permet de créer des ambiances enjôleuses et séduisantes et confère à l'ensemble une sensation d'espace. Fraccaroli a opté pour une structure polyvalente qui sépare le salon et la chambre grâce à une cloison vitrée verte. La séparation des deux environnements se fait par un jeu varié de couleurs qui module le design de l'espace à sa guise. Cet effet accentue l'aspect utilitaire de l'appartement et correspond aux besoins de la personne qui l'habite, à la recherche d'efficacité et de sens pratique au sein d'un environnement tout en élégance sous le signe du luxe, profession oblige.

Dieses Appartement verbindet einige ursprüngliche Elemente mit der Kunst des Architekten. Das gefärbte Glas sticht besonders hervor und unterstreicht das anheimelnde Ambiente, während es gleichzeitig die Weite des Raumes verstärkt. Fraccaroli hat sich für eine wandlungsfähige Struktur entschieden, die Wohn- und Schlafzimmer durch eine Trennwand aus grünem Glas abschirmt. Auf diese Weise wird die Trennung der beiden Wohnbereiche durch verschiedene Lichtpunkte erzeugt. Dieser Effekt unterstreicht die Zweckmäßigkeit des Appartements und entspricht den Anforderungen seiner Bewohnerin, die innerhalb einer eleganten Umgebung auch Effizienz und Annehmlichkeit zu schätzen weiß, verbunden mit einem gewissen Luxus, der ihrem Berufsbild entspricht.

The kitchen, which is equipped with the most advanced technology, reflects a futurist and aseptic aesthetic.

La cuisine, avec son équipement à la pointe de la technique, dégage une esthétique futuriste et aseptique.

Die Küche, die mit modernster Technologie ausgestattet wurde, weist eine futuristische, und eher herbe Ästhetik auf.

Apartment in Margareten
Appartement à Margareten
Appartement in Margarethen

Vienna, Austria

The top floor of a building in Vienna's Margareten district was converted into four tiny apartments. To compensate for the smallness of the apartments, a common area, placed next to the stairs, is used for storage, as a laundry room, or to expand the social area as needed. The absence of interior walls lowered costs still further, as well as corresponding with the design concept. In this case, the finishes are the same polished concrete and glass that serve as connecting elements. In one of the apartments, a concrete wall divides the bathroom from a series of cubes that contain the sleeping quarter and a home office. This yellow structure incorporates a staircase that pulls out, like a puzzle piece, to provide access to the these rooms. The office, which receives natural light from long and narrow openings in the concrete walls, remains out of sight from the rest of the living space.

Le dernier étage d'un bâtiment du quartier viennois Margareten a été transformé en quatre petits appartements. Pour remédier à leur taille réduite, une zone commune, placée à côté des escaliers est utilisée comme aire de rangement, de laverie ou pour agrandir l'espace de réception au gré des besoins. L'absence de murs intérieurs correspond au concept du design et permet de réduire les dépenses. Dans ce cas, les matériaux de finition sont le béton et le verre servant aussi d'éléments de connexion. Dans l'un des appartements, un mur de béton sépare la salle de bains d'une série de cubes abritant les chambres et le bureau. Cette structure jaune héberge un escalier escamotable que l'on sort comme un morceau de puzzle pour accéder à ces chambres. Ce dernier reçoit la lumière naturelle grâce à de longues ouvertures étroites dans le mur de béton, mais n'est pas visible depuis le reste de l'espace de vie.

Die obere Etage eines Gebäudes im Wiener Margarethenviertel wurde in vier kleine Appartements umgebaut. Um die geringe Größe der Appartements zu kompensieren, wird ein gemeinschaftlich genutzter Raum neben den Treppen als Lagerraum und Wäschekammer genutzt, kann aber bei Bedarf auch den Wohnbereich erweitern. Durch das Fehlen von Innenwänden konnten die Kosten niedrig gehalten werden. In diesem Fall dienen der polierte Beton und Glaselemente als verbindende Elemente. In einem der Appartements teilt eine Betonwand die Zimmer in eine Reihe von Quadern, die das Schlafquartier und ein Heimbüro enthalten. Diese gelbe Struktur enthält eine ausziehbare Treppe, die Zugang zum Schlafzimmer und Büro bietet. Das Büro wird durch die langen und engen Öffnungen in den Betonwänden mit Tageslicht versorgt und ist gleichzeitig vom restlichen Wohnbereich abgetrennt.

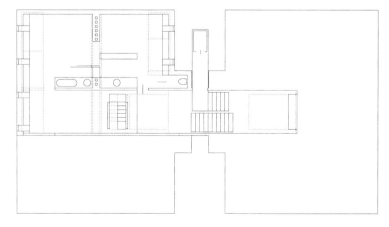

› Plan Plan Grundriss

William P. Bruder

Mad River Boat Trips

Jackson, United States

This building was designed to serve three different functions, with separate private and public areas but simple connections between them. The first unit to be put up was a warehouse for the boats and accessories like waterproof clothing, ropes, and tools. The second unit is a small customer-service section, with a reception area where the public can relax and seek information. The third unit comprises the private quarters, divided into rooms for the workers and a residence for the owner, as well as a library and study room. In spite of the considerable functional diversity, the architect produced a logical, orderly, and compact layout. Simple wood construction techniques were used for the building. The upper levels are suspended from a beam arrangement, which permits greater flexibility on the first floor.

Ce bâtiment a été conçu pour répondre à trois diverses fonctions accompagnées d'aires publiques et privées séparées, reliées simplement entre elles. La première unité comprend un entrepôt pour bateaux et accessoires à l'instar d'habits imperméables, de cordes et d'outils. La deuxième unité est une petite zone de service clientèle, dotée d'une aire de réception où le public peut à la fois se renseigner et se détendre. La troisième unité abrite les quartiers privés, partagés entre les chambres pour le personnel et une résidence pour le propriétaire ainsi qu'une bibliothèque et une salle de lecture. Malgré la grande diversité des fonctions, l'architecte a réalisé un plan logique, bien agencé et compact. Le bâtiment utilise des constructions simples en bois. Les niveaux supérieurs sont suspendus à un système de poutre qui permet de moduler facilement le premier étage.

Dieses Gebäude sollte drei verschiedenen Funktionen dienen und dabei separate, private und öffentliche Bereiche aufweisen. Beim ersten Gebäudeteil handelt es sich um ein Lager für Boote und das Zubehör wie z.B. Wasserschutzbekleidung, Seile und Werkzeuge. Der Zweite ist ein kleineres Gebäude mit der Rezeption, in dem die Besucher sich entspannen und um Information bitten können. Im dritten Teil liegen die Privatquartiere, die wiederum aufgeteilt wurden in Zimmer für die Arbeiter, ein Wohnhaus für den Eigentümer sowie Bibliothek und Studierzimmer. Trotz der beachtlich funktionellen Vielfalt hat der Architekt ein logisches und kompaktes Layout entworfen. Das Gebäude wurde mit einfachen Holzkonstruktionen errichtet. Die oberen Ebenen werden von einer Balkenkonstruktion gehalten, die eine hohe Flexibilität auf dem ersten Stock ermöglicht. Zwei besondere Balken aus Holz und Stahl stützen die östliche Glasfassade.

This complex is evocative of the region's typical ranches and recalls Wyoming's pioneering roots; its simple elegance commands attention in the undefined surroundings.

Ce complexe évoque les ranchs typiques de la région et rappelle les racines pionnières de Wyoming. Cette élégance simple est l'attraction de cette zone indéfinie.

Die Anlage Mad River Boat Trips erinnert an die typischen Farmhäuser der Gegend. Ihre einfache Eleganz in der undefinierten Umgebung sticht dabei besonders hervor.

› Ground floor   Rez-de-chaussée   Erdgeschoss

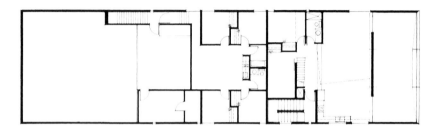

› First floor   Premier étage   Erstes Obergeschoss

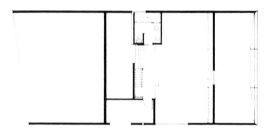

› Second floor   Deuxième étage   Zweites Obergeschoss

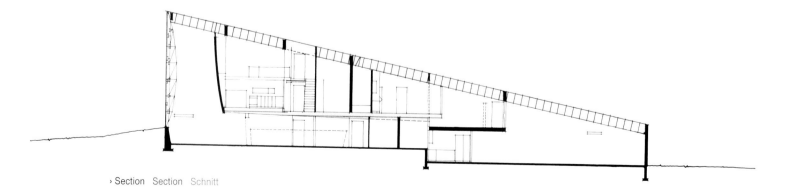

› Section   Section   Schnitt

The lighting create dramatic effects; the reception counter, for example, features colored spotlights.

L'éclairage génére des effets spectaculaires à l'instar du comptoir de la réception équipé de spots de couleur.

Besonders in den Arbeitsbereichen wurden dramatische Effekte mit Licht geschaffen, so z.B. auf dem Tisch an der Rezeption, der mit Farbspots beschienen wird.

In spite of the considerable functional diversity, the architect produced a logical, orderly and compact layout.

Malgré la grande diversité fonctionnelle, l'architecte a conçu un plan logique, bien agencé et compact

Trotz der beachtlichen funktionellen Vielfalt hat der Architekt ein logisches, gut geordnetes und kompaktes Layout entworfen.

The owners' residence is located on the upper level and is equipped with a library and study

La résidence du propriétaire, située au niveau supérieur, est équipée d'une bibliothèque et d'un studio..

Die Wohnung der Besitzer liegt auf der oberen Etage und verfügt über eine Bibliothek und ein Studierzimmer.

Studio in Sant Cugat
Studio à Sant Cugat
Studio in Sant Cugat

Sant Cugat, Spain

The aim of the renovation of this apartment was to create a space with a separate room, which serves as an office. The architect opted for a solution whereby the office doubled up as a guest room. For this reason, a table with two rolling table-legs was fixed on a rail on the wall, which allows an easy displacement when the room has to be used as guest room or second bedroom. The sofa converts into a bed where the former backrest serves as the headboard. The small dimensions of the space did not allow for more than one bookcase, which was fixed below the window, to complete the office. Bright colors and designer furniture make the space a modern, innovative home.

La rénovation de cet appartement a pour but de créer un espace doté d'une pièce séparée en guise de bureau. L'architecte a opté pour un bureau à double fonction puisqu'il sert aussi de chambre d'amis. A cet effet, il a créé une table dont deux pieds sur roulettes sont fixés à un rail mural afin de la déplacer facilement lorsque la pièce fait office de chambre d'amis ou deuxième chambre à coucher. Le divan est convertible en lit avec le dossier latéral en guise de tête de lit. Les dimensions réduites de l'espace ne permettent d'installer qu'une seule bibliothèque, fixée en l'occurrence sous la fenêtre pour parachever le bureau. Couleurs vives et meubles design font de cet espace une habitation moderne et innovante.

Ziel bei der Renovierung dieses Apartments war es, einen Raum mit einem separaten Büro einzurichten. Der Architekt hat sich für eine Lösung entschieden, bei der das Büro auch als Gästezimmer genutzt werden kann. Dafür wurde ein Tisch mit zwei Tischbeinen auf Rollen an einer Schiene an der Wand befestigt, so dass er leicht weg geschoben werden kann. Das Sofa kann zum Bett umfunktioniert werden, wobei die Rückenlehne als Kopfbrett dient. Die begrenzten Dimensionen des Raumes ließen nur Platz für ein Regal, das unter dem Fenster angebracht ist. Leuchtende Farben und Designermöbel verwandeln den Raum in ein modernes, innovatives Zuhause.

Due to the limited surface area, special furniture was designed, including this bookcase, integrated into the backrest of the sofa.

Pour pallier la limitation de l'espace, des meubles ont été spécialement conçus, à l'instar de cette bibliothèque, intégrée dans le dossier du divan.

Um den geringen Raum so gut wie möglich zu nutzen, wurden Sonderanfertigungen entworfen, wie z.B. dieses Regal, das die Rückwand des Sofas ausmacht.

Attic in Andorra
Attique en Andorre
Dachgeschoss in Andorra

Andorra la Vella, Andorra

One of the main objectives of the project is to allow the maximum transparency in a space where more than two thirds of the façade communicate with a dividing wall or interior patios. Therefore, it is all about obtaining great fluency of spaces, within the confines of a housing project. The plan responds to the needs of a single person who wants to enjoy the whole space during the week, whilst welcoming lots of visitors at the weekend. The room that was the living room has been voluntarily eliminated since the idea was to convert the whole apartment into a living room, in which the most ample room is the kitchen - dining room. The wall - library in the entrance creates a circular space between the day zone and the night zone. On one hand it works as a place to receive visitors and allows a glimpse of the exterior through a small opening, and on the other hand it embraces the reading and work zone.

L'un des objectifs majeurs de ce projet est d'obtenir un maximum de transparence spatiale dans un volume où plus des deux tiers de la façade communiquent avec une cloison ou des patios intérieurs. L'idée est donc de créer une grande fluidité entre les espaces au sein d'un projet d'habitation. Le plan correspond aux besoins d'une seule personne dont le souhait est de profiter de tout l'espace pendant la semaine et d'accueillir un grand nombre de visiteurs durant le week-end. La pièce servant autrefois de salon a été supprimée sciemment pour réaliser l'idée de convertir tout l'appartement en un seul salon où la cuisine-salle à manger occupe une place essentielle. Le mur - bibliothèque de l'entrée crée un espace circulaire entre la zone de jour et la zone de nuit. Il fait office, d'une part de lieu de réception des visiteurs offrant un aperçu de l'extérieur grâce à une petite ouverture et d'autre part, il comprend la zone de lecture et de travail.

Eine der wichtigsten Vorgaben in diesem Projekt war, so viel Transparenz wie möglich in einem Raum zu schaffen, dessen Fassade zu zwei Dritteln mit Trennwänden oder Innenhöfen verbunden ist. Es sollten also miteinander verbundene Räume innerhalb der Grenzen eines Wohnungsprojektes entstehen. Der Plan entspricht den Bedürfnissen einer Einzelperson, die am Wochenende aber durchaus auch Besuch empfangen möchte. Das ehemalige Wohnzimmer wurde als solches aufgelöst, da man das gesamte Appartement in einen Wohnraum verwandeln wollte, bei dem das größte Zimmer die Küche mit Esszimmer darstellt. Die Wandbibliothek im Eingang schafft eine runde Abtrennung zwischen Tages- und Nachtbereich. Auf der einen Seite dient sie dazu, Besucher zu empfangen und auf der anderen trennt sie Lese- und Arbeitsbereich von außen ab.

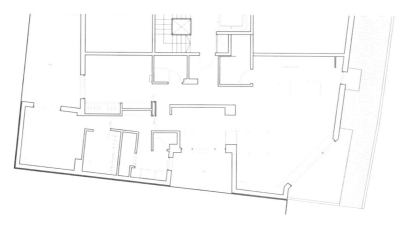

› Plan Plan Grundriss

Apartment in Fusina Street
Appartement de la rue Fusina
Appartement in der Fusina Strasse

Barcelona, Spain

The architect Gustavo Barba was commissioned to transform this small apartment into a friendly, modern dwelling to provide a comfortable space for working at home. The layout is an open distribution where only the bedroom and service areas are separated by a door. In the main room, a large wooden board is fixed along the whole length of the side wall, providing room for storing books and working equipment, without occupying to much space. The same wooden board serves as a desktop where the computer is placed, supplemented by chrome furniture and chrome accessories. Solid wooden ceiling beams and brick walls combined with the gray floors guarantee a space full of character in this post-industrial apartment. The large windows situated along the side walls allow the entire space to be flooded with natural light.

L'architecte Gustavo Barba a été chargé de convertir ce petit appartement en une résidence conviviale et moderne pour y travailler à domicile. Le plan s'articule autour d'une distribution spatiale ouverte où seules la chambre à coucher et la zone de services sont séparées par une porte. Dans la pièce principale, un grand élément de bois est fixé sur toute la longueur du mur latéral faisant office d'espace de rangement de livres et d'équipement professionnel sans prendre trop de place. Cette large bordure de bois sert aussi de dessus de bureau pour y poser l'ordinateur, agrémenté de meubles et d'accessoires en chrome. Les poutres de bois massives du plafond et les murs de briques, conjugués aux sols gris, signent l'espace de cet appartement post-industriel. Les grandes fenêtres situées le long des murs latéraux inondent la totalité de l'espace de lumière naturelle.

Der Architekt Gustavo Barba wurde mit dem Umbau dieses kleinen Appartements in Barcelona beauftragt. Vorgabe war ein freundlicher, moderner Wohnraum, in dem man gleichzeitig auch von zu Hause aus arbeiten können sollte. Der Grundriss zeigt eine offene Verteilung, bei der nur Schlafzimmer und Nutzräume durch eine Tür abgetrennt sind. Im großen Zimmer bietet ein über die gesamte Länge der Seitenwand angebrachtes Holzbrett Raum für Bücher und Arbeitsgeräte, ohne zu viel Platz in Anspruch zu nehmen. Das selbe Brett dient auch als Schreibtisch, auf dem der Computer steht. Chrommöbel und Chromaccessoires geben dem Ganzen die nötigen Akzente. Solide Holzdeckenbalken und Ziegelwände bilden gemeinsam mit dem grauen Boden ein beeindruckendes Ambiente in diesem post-industriellen Appartement.

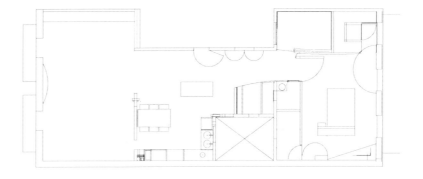

› Plan Plan Grundriss

The plan has an open distribution, where a half long brick wall serves to visually separate the dining area from the rest of the space.

Le plan présente une distribution spatiale ouverte où un mur de brique à mi-hauteur sert de séparation visuelle entre la salle à manger et le reste de l'espace.

Der Grundriss sieht eine offene Aufteilung vor, bei der eine halbhohe Ziegelwand den Essbereich vom Rest des Raumes abtrennt.

House in Esplugues
Maison à Esplugues
Haus in Esplugues

Barcelona, Spain

In this house the upper level is used as a working zone; the space was divided into two by a furniture piece that can also be used for storage. This way, the family can also enjoy the space for leisure and for relaxing. Everything in the house is integrated but separated from the bedrooms, living room and kitchen, situated in the lower floor. The project for the space was designed with the idea that all members of the family could work in unison. Therefore we see the tables placed in a square. The furniture chosen was very important in order to achieve the objective. It was devised so as to maintain the advantages of office furniture whilst giving the zone a homely feeling.

Dans cette maison le niveau supérieur a été designé comme zone de travail; qui a été divisée en deux espaces avec un meuble bas qui est utile pour le stockage. La famille peut aussi utiliser cet espace pour le loisir et la détente où tout est intégré tout en étant séparé des chambres à coucher du salon et de la cuisine, qui sont dans le niveau inferieur. L'idée de ce projet était de concevoir un espace où tous les membres de la famille puissent travailler en cœur, d'où la disposition des tables en carré. Le mobilier sélectionné joue un rôle primordial dans la réalisation de cet objectif. Conçu avec tous les avantages du mobilier de bureau, il confère aussi à l'espace une sensation de confort et de convivialité.

In diesem Haus wurde das gesammte obere Stockwerk den Arbeitsräumen gewidmed. Der Raum wurde durch ein Möbelstück in zwei Bereiche unterteilt, welches zugleich als Ablagefläche dient. So kann die Familie den Raum auch während der Freizeit und zur Entspannung nutzen. Alles im Haus ist miteinander verbunden, aber gleichzeitig getrennt von den Schlafzimmern, dem Wohnzimmer und der Küche, die im unteren Stockwerk liegen. Dadurch wird der Raum optimal genutzt. Die Idee dahinter war, dass alle Mitglieder der Familie gemeinsam arbeiten können. Deshalb sind die Tische in Quadratform angelegt. Die gewählten Möbel sollen ebenfalls diesem Ziel dienen. Obwohl es sich um praktische Büromöbel handelt, fühlt man sich dennoch gleich zu Hause.

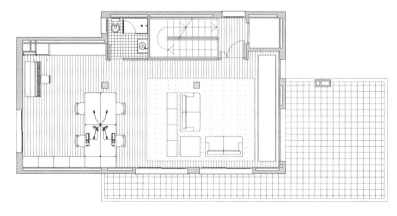

› Plan   Plan   Grundriss

The selection of the furniture is important for the specific needs of the inhabitants.

Il est primordial de choisir les meubles en fonction des besoins personnels des habitants.

Die Auswahl der Möbel ist auf die besonderen Anforderungen der Bewohner ausgerichtet.

Loft in Tribeca
Loft à Tribeca
Loft in Tribeca

New York, United States

The first step in the renovation of this loft was the elimination of as many interior walls as possible in order to create a greater feeling of space and light. Light, flexible materials and design elements were used to fulfill the project's requirements while preserving the proportions of the space that had previously been created. The guest room, for example, consists of a foldout bed and two drapes that define the space. Materials such as ebony, shiny drapes, and Peruvian ceramics have created a very elegant and sophisticated atmosphere. The choice of furniture was inspired by the client's extensive collection of art and photographs dominated by lively, intense colors. A palette of soft colors and earth tones was chosen, and the furniture was confined to a few pieces that would have a great impact on the space.

La rénovation de ce loft a commencé par l'élimination du plus grand nombre de murs intérieurs pour accroître la sensation d'espace et de lumière. Eclairage, matériaux flexibles et éléments design sont employés pour répondre à ces critères tout en conservant les proportions de l'espace préexistant. Dans la chambre d'amis, par exemple, deux lits pliants et deux tentures meublent et définissent l'espace. Matériaux tels que l'ivoire, tentures soyeuses et céramiques péruviennes ponctuent l'ambiance d'une subtile élégance. Des meubles ont été choisis pour mettre en valeur l'importante collection d'art et de photographies du client aux couleurs intenses et vives. Une palette de couleurs douces et de nuances ocres accentue l'impact du mobilier, limité à quelques pièces maîtresses, sur l'espace.

Der erste Schritt bei der Renovierung dieses Lofts bestand im Abriss so vieler Innenwände wie möglich, um ein Gefühl von Weite und Licht zu schaffen. Leichte, flexible Materialien und Designelemente wurden eingesetzt, um den Anforderungen des Projektes zu entsprechen. Dabei sind aber die Proportionen des Raums, der vorher geschaffen wurde, beibehalten. Das Gästezimmer besteht z.B. aus einer Klappcouch und zwei Vorhängen, die den Raum bestimmen. Materialien wie Ebenholz, schimmernde Vorhänge und peruanische Keramik sorgen für ein elegantes und anspruchsvolles Ambiente. Die Wahl der Möbel wurde durch die große Kunst- und Fotosammlung des Kunden bestimmt, die von lebhaften, intensiven Farben durchdrungen ist. Eine Palette von sanften Farben und Erdtönen wurde ausgewählt und die Möbel auf ein paar wenige Einzelteile beschränkt.

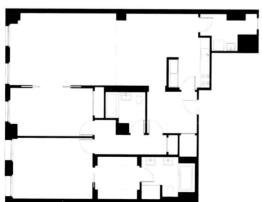
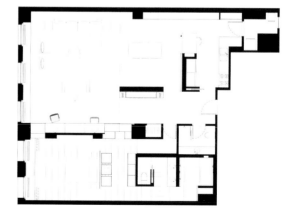

› Plans Plans Grundrisse

Innauer House
Maison Innauer
Innauer Haus

Dornbirn, Austria

This family house in Vorarlberg, Austria, was supervised by the architect Oskar Leo Kaufmann and accommodates a residence and an office at the same time. The clients desired a flexible, open home with an office that had to be easily accessed from various points in the apartment. At the same time, the work area had to be sufficiently isolated to avoid any interference with other activities. The architect opted for an open plan set in the 3,000-sq.-ft expanse, in order to guarantee the necessary spatial flexibility. The materials used for the floors, ceilings and walls are concrete, light wood and stainless steel, creating a modern, industrial atmosphere that contrasts with the red furniture in the working area. Translucent doors and room dividers allow natural light to penetrating the space during the day. The house is made of a univalve concrete construction, while all the ceilings and walls are free of any additional superstructure.

L'architecte Oskar Leo Kaufmann a construit cette maison de famille à Vorarlberg, en Autriche. Elle englobe une résidence et un bureau. Les clients voulaient une maison ouverte et flexible dotée d'un bureau facilement accessible en même temps de plusieurs endroits de l'appartement. L'espace de travail devait être suffisamment isolé du reste de l'appartement pour ne pas être gêné par d'autres activités. Pour assurer la flexibilité spatiale nécessaire, l'architecte a opté pour un plan ouvert sur une superficie de 280 m². Au sol, au plafond et sur les murs, les matériaux employés sont le béton, le bois léger et l'acier inoxydable pour créer une atmosphère moderne et industrielle contrastant avec le mobilier rouge de l'espace bureau. Portes et cloisons translucides permettent à la lumière naturelle de pénétrer l'espace pendant la journée. La maison est construite en béton cellulaire, les plafonds et les murs sont dépourvus de tout revêtement supplémentaire.

Dieses Familienhaus in Vorarlberg wurde vom Architekten Oskar Leo Kaufmann entworfen und bietet Platz für eine Wohnung und ein Büro. Die Kunden wünschten sich einen flexiblen, offenen Wohnbereich mit einem Büro, in das man von verschiedenen Punkten des Appartements aus eintreten kann. Gleichzeitig sollte der Arbeitsbereich jedoch auch entsprechend abgeschirmt bleiben. Der Architekt entschied sich für einen offenen Grundriss für die knapp 280 m² Grundfläche, um die entsprechende räumliche Flexibilität zu gewährleisten. Für Böden, Wände und Decken wurden Beton, leichtes Holz und Edelstahl verwendet, was ein modernes, industrielles Ambiente schafft, das mit den roten Möbeln im Arbeitsbereich kontrastiert. Durchsichtige Türen und Raumteiler ermöglichen den Einfall von natürlichem Tageslicht. Das Haus ist auf einem festen Betonfundament gebaut, Wände und Decken müssen keine besondere Stützfunktion ausüben.

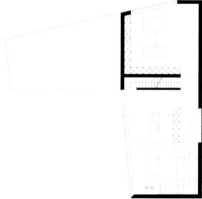

› Plan Plan Grundriss

The materials used for the floors, ceilings and walls creating a modern, industrial atmosphere.

Les matériaux utilisés pour les sols, plafonds et murs créent une ambiance moderne et industrielle.

Das Material, das für die Böden, Decken und Wände genutzt wurde, schafft ein modernes, gewerblich angehauchtes Ambiente.

Attic in Barcelona
Attique à Barcelone
Dachgeschoss in Barcelona

Barcelona, Spain

In this duplex, designed by and for an interior designer, partitions were especially important in separating the working area from the living room. A rectangular configuration, with a terrace at one end, required the living area and design studio to be set within a shared space. The bedroom was situated upstairs for privacy. The work area was assigned to the far end of the apartment, with the advantage of a terrace that provides light, privacy, and tranquility. Two half-height partitions—fitted with bookcases on the studio side—were installed to establish a clear separation from the living room, kitchen, and dining area, creating the sensation of depth and continuity. In order to provide this area with light, a glass ceiling was introduced on the upper level to filter the sunlight that pours in through the skylight in the bedroom ceiling.

Dans ce duplex, conçu par un designer d'intérieur, les cloisons jouent un rôle décisif dans la séparation entre l'aire de travail et le salon. Dû à une configuration rectangulaire dotée d'une terrasse à une extrémité, le salon et le studio de design doivent se partager l'espace. Pour plus d'intimité, la chambre à coucher est placée à l'étage. L'espace de travail est relégué au bout de l'appartement bénéficiant de la terrasse qui lui confère lumière, intimité et calme. Deux cloisons à mi-hauteur –aménagées d'étagères du côté studio– instaurent une séparation nette entre le salon, la cuisine et la salle à manger, créant une sensation de profondeur et de continuité. Un plafond de verre installé à l'étage supérieur, inonde cet espace de lumière. Il filtre la lumière qui pénètre par le velux dans la chambre à coucher.

In diesem Zweifamilienhaus, das von und für einen Innenarchitekten entworfen wurde, sollte vor allem der Arbeitsbereich vom Wohnbereich getrennt werden. Die rechteckige Konfiguration weist an einem Ende auf eine Terrasse, weshalb Wohnbereich und Designstudio in einem gemeinsamen Raum untergebracht werden mussten. Das Schlafzimmer wurde nach oben verlegt. Der Arbeitsbereich liegt an einem Ende des Appartements, sodass die Terrasse jetzt Licht, Privatsphäre und Ruhe bietet. Zwei Trennwände auf halber Höhe (mit Regalen auf der Seite des Studios) bieten eine klare Trennung von Wohnbereich, Küche und Esszimmer. Um diesen Teil mit Licht auszustatten, wurde weiter oben eine Glasdecke eingezogen, die das Tageslicht filtert, das durch das Dachfenster im Schlafzimmer einfällt.

A metal staircase leads to the bedroom, which is situated upstairs to guarantee privacy.

Un escalier de métal dessert la chambre à coucher, située en haut pour un maximum d'intimité.

Eine Metalltreppe führt nach oben in das Schlafzimmer, wo Privatsphäre gewährleistet ist.

Two half-height partitions that double as bookcases on the studio side were put up to create a clear separation from the living room, kitchen, and dining area.

Deux cloisons à mi-hauteur qui font aussi office de bibliothèque du côté studio, créent une séparation nette entre le salon, la cuisine et la salle à manger.

Zwei halbhohe Trennwände, die auf Studioseite als Bücherregale dienen, bilden eine klare Trennung von Wohnzimmer, Küche und Essbereich.

Dwelling Lipschutz-Jones
Maison Lipschutz-Jones
Haus Lipschutz-Jones

New York, United States

This apartment was designed for a pair of Wall Street stockbrokers. The clients wanted a flexible, open home with a work area to house their computer and communication systems, so that they could monitor the market at any time. The office had to be easily visible from various points in the apartment, while being sufficiently isolated to avoid interference with other activities. A high narrow passage connects the rooms and partitions off the different areas. The kitchen is on one side, with a bedroom above it, while the office lies to the other side, below the master bathroom. This means that the work area is separated from the bedrooms but can be seen from the kitchen and central corridor. A wide range of materials, including maple wood, marble, granite, and translucent glass, was used in all the rooms to create a home with a strong visual impact.

Cet appartement a été conçu pour un couple d'agents de change de Wall Street. Les clients désiraient un logement ouvert et modulable, doté d'un espace de travail pour accueillir leurs systèmes d'ordinateurs et de communication, pour consulter le marché en permanence. Le bureau doit être facilement visible de divers angles de l'appartement tout en étant suffisamment isolé pour permettre d'autres activités sans gêner. Un long étroit passage relie les pièces et les espaces cloisonnés entre eux. La cuisine est placée d'un côté, avec une chambre au-dessus et le bureau se trouve de l'autre côté sous la salle de bains principale. L'espace travail est donc séparé des chambres mais peut être vu depuis la cuisine et du couloir central. Une large palette de matériaux, déclinant bois d'érable, granit et verre translucide, appliquée à toutes les pièces, confère un fort impact visuel à cette espace de vie.

Das Appartement wurde von zwei Wall Street Maklern entworfen. Die Kunden wünschten sich einen flexiblen, offenen Wohnbereich mit integriertem Arbeitsbereich, um ihre Computer unterbringen und den Markt auch von hier aus beobachten zu können. Das Büro sollte von verschiedenen Punkten im Appartement aus sichtbar sein, gleichzeitig aber von anderen Aktivitäten entsprechend abgeschirmt bleiben. Ein hoher, enger Flur verbindet die Räume und die Abtrennungen der verschiedenen Bereiche miteinander. Die Küche befindet sich auf der einen Seite, das Schlafzimmer direkt darüber. Das Büro liegt direkt gegenüber unter dem großen Badezimmer. Dadurch ist der Arbeitsbereich von den Schlafzimmern getrennt, kann aber von der Küche und vom zentralen Flur aus eingesehen werden. Eine Reihe verschiedenartiger Materialien, wie Ahornholz, Marmor, Granit und Glas, machen das Appartement zu einem besonderen Blickfang.

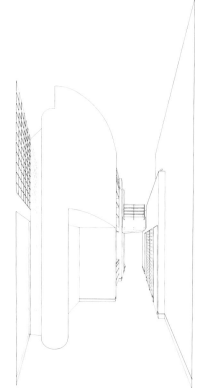

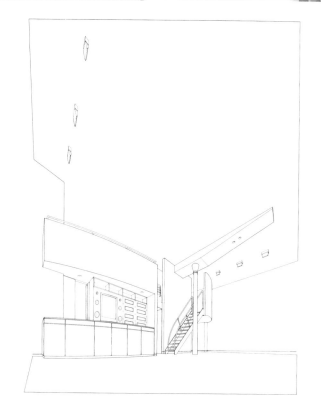

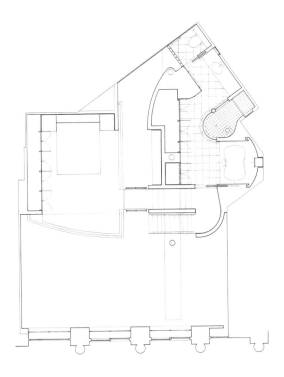

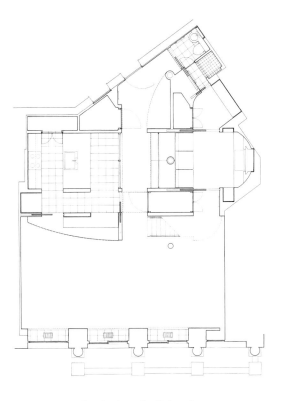

› First floor   Premier étage   Erstes Obergeschoss

› Ground floor   Rez-de-chaussée   Erdgeschoss

This room contains sophisticated computer and communication technology that allows the residents to monitor the stock market at all times.

La maison est équipée d'un système d'ordinateurs et de communication de pointe pour permettre aux propriétaires de consulter le marché de la bourse à tout moment.

In diesem Zimmer ist die IT-Hardware untergebracht, dadurch können die Bewohner den Aktienmarkt jederzeit im Auge behalten.

This extensive, flexible space has been partitioned with extremely striking, panelled walls.

Cet espace, vaste et flexible est cloisonné par des murs lambrissés d'une très belle esthétique visuelle.

Dieser weitläufige Raum wurde mit wunderschön getäfelten Wänden unterteilt.

House in Rosoman Street
Maison de la rue Rosoman
Haus in der Rosoman Strasse

London, United Kingdom

This apartment was created as a home and studio for two interior designers; the industrial nature of the building was modified by introducing woodwork and finishings that give the home a more contemporary feel. From the outset, a great effort was made to preserve the feeling of light and space and create a work area and meeting rooms without destroying the sense of intimacy. An imaginary line divides the layout down the center. On one side, there is a wide, flexible area for living and working, and on the other the master bedroom with a bathroom. Two translucent screens near the entrance are normally folded back to allow fluidity of movement. By sliding one screen across, the passageway becomes a meeting room, so, business can be conducted without visitors seeing the private home. A hidden door in the entrance hall leads to the bathroom, which can also be divided, with one area being kept private if desired.

Cet appartement réunit le domicile et le studio de deux designers d'intérieur. Ebénisterie et habillages ont modifié la nature industrielle de l'édifice, l'imprimant d'une ambiance plus contemporaine. Dés le départ, il a été primordial de préserver la sensation d'espace et de lumière et de créer une aire de travail et de réunion en conservant une certaine intimité. Une ligne imaginaire divise le plan vers le centre. D'un côté, il y a un vaste espace modulable pour y vivre et travailler, et de l'autre, la chambre à coucher avec salle de bains. A l'entrée, deux paravents translucides se replient pour plus de liberté de mouvement. En faisant coulisser l'un des deux, le hall de passage devient salle de réunion, les affaires peuvent avoir lieu sans que les visiteurs aperçoivent la sphère privée. Dans le hall d'entrée, une porte cachée conduit à la salle de bains, divisible à son tour pour garder une partie privée, si nécessaire.

Dieses Appartement wurde als Wohn- und Arbeitsplatz für zwei Innenarchitekten konzipiert. Holzarbeiten und Details lockern den vormals gewerblichen Bau auf und verleihen der Wohnung ein moderneres Aussehen. Von Beginn an wurde darauf geachtet, das Gefühl von Licht und Raum beizubehalten und einen Arbeitsbereich sowie Konferenzräume einzurichten, ohne den Eindruck von Privatsphäre zu stören. Eine imaginäre Linie teilt den Grundriss in der Mitte. Auf der einen Seite gibt es einen breiten, flexiblen Wohn- und Arbeitsbereich, auf der anderen ein großes Schlafzimmer mit Bad. Zwei durchsichtige Trennwände im Eingangsbereich werden normalerweise zurückgeklappt, um den Durchgang zu erleichtern. Wird eine davon vorgeschoben, verwandelt sich der Flur in einen Konferenzraum. So können hier Besucher empfangen werden, ohne dass sie Einblick in den Wohnbereich erhalten. Eine verborgene Tür in der Eingangshalle führt zum Bad, das ebenfalls geteilt werden kann.

› Plans Plans Grundrisse

The guest room contains a fold-away bed, which is one of many devices that enhance this flexible, multiuse home.

La chambre d'amis contient un lit pliant escamotable, un des nombreux aspects qui souligne la polyvalence de cette habitation.

Im Gästezimmer steht ein Schlafsofa, eines der unzähligen Details dieses flexiblen Multifunktionshauses.

D2 House
Maison D2
D2-Haus

Plentzia, Spain

In the El Abanico complex, between the coast and the locality of Plentzia, facing south and with unbeatable views of the estuary and the valley that forms it, we come across a project of two independent terraced houses up for sale. From the landscaped deck and through a central patio we reach the daytime zone of the house, the sitting room, dining room, and kitchen. On the lower floor we find the bedrooms and bathrooms. On both floors have outdoor terrace and we can access the garden from the lower floor bedrooms. The home opens up to the landscape on the south face. It's a more visual and contemplative connection than a physical one, conditioned, obviously, by the difficulties posed by developing on such sloping land, and by the new type of relationship that we think about establishing for the dweller with their natural or rural environment, the one that he or she is returning to colonize.

Dans le complexe d'El Abanico, entre la côte et la localité de Plentzia, face au sud avec une vue imprenable sur l'estuaire et sa vallée, il y a deux maisons adjacentes et indépendantes mises en vente. Après avoir traversé le ponton paysagér et un patio central, nous accédons à la zone de jour de la maison, le salon, la salle de séjour et la cuisine. L'étage inférieur héberge les chambres à coucher et les salles de bains. Les deux étages débouchent sur des terrasses extérieures et les chambres situées à l'étage inférieur donnent sur le jardin. Du côté sud, la maison s'ouvre sur le paysage, dans un but plus visuel et contemplatif que physique vu la difficulté de construire sur un terrain en pente et la relation à établir entre le propriétaire et la nature environnante qui dépend de ses désirs personnels.

In der Wohnanlage El Abanico, zwischen Küste und Plentzia, steht ein Projekt zum Verkauf mit zwei voneinander unabhängigen Häusern mit Terrasse. Von dem begrünten Deck aus und durch einen zentralen Innenhof erreicht man den Tagesbereich des Hauses: Wohnzimmer, Esszimmer und Küche. Unten befinden sich dann Schlaf- und Badezimmer. Auf beiden Stockwerken gibt es Terrassen und den Garten erreicht man durch die Schlafzimmer unten. Das Haus weist auf die herrliche Landschaft an der Südseite. Dabei handelt es sich mehr um eine visuelle Verbindung als eine physikalische, begründet durch die Hanglage und die neue Art von Beziehung, die der Bewohner mit der umgebenden Landschaft eingehen möchte.

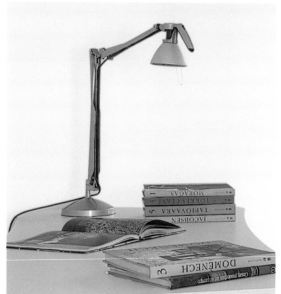

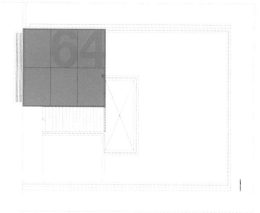

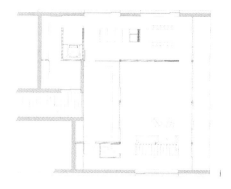

› Plans Plans Grundrisse

Jeremy King

Atelier in Shepherd's Bush
Atelier à Shepherd's Bush
Atelier in Shepherd's Bush

London, United Kingdom

The goal for the renovation of this small apartment was an efficient home and workspace for one person that provided the maximum amount of storage room. A long storage unit was hung on the side wall, thus maintaining a feeling of continuity while respecting the room's original proportions. It contains clothing, household appliances, and, most importantly, a drawing table and office area. The materials' neutral textures and colors minimize the impact of the renovation. Afromosia-wood floorboards connect the two spaces and add a warm touch. The bedroom and kitchen furnishings are painted white to blend with the walls. The subtle refurbishment of this interior—with warm materials such as wood, natural fabrics for the chairs and drapes, and well-placed splashes of color—respects the original personality of the building.

La restauration de ce petit appartement doit permettre de créer un logement et un bureau idéaux pour une personne ainsi qu'un maximum d'espace de rangement. Un grand module de rangement a été accroché le long du mur latéral pour ne pas nuire à la sensation de continuité tout en respectant les proportions initiales de la pièce. Il contient des habits, des ustensiles ménagers et surtout une planche à dessin et un espace bureau. La texture neutre des matériaux et les couleurs réduisent l'impact de la restauration. Un parquet en bois d'afromosia relie les deux espaces en ajoutant une touche chaleureuse. Le mobilier de la chambre à coucher et de la cuisine est peint en blanc en harmonie avec les murs. La rénovation ingénieuse de cet intérieur –grâce à des matériaux chauds comme le bois, aux tissus naturels des chaises et à des tentures et des touches de couleurs bien placées– respecte la personnalité initiale de cet édifice.

Das Ziel der Renovierung dieses kleinen Appartements war ein effizienter Wohn- und Arbeitsplatz für eine Person mit größtmöglichem Stauraum. Eine große Lagereinheit wurde an eine Seitenwand angefügt. Das verleiht dieser Struktur ein Gefühl von Kontinuität, während die ursprünglichen Proportionen des Zimmers beibehalten wurden. Darin verstaut werden die Bekleidung, Haushaltsgeräte, ein Zeichentisch sowie ein Bürobereich. Die neutrale Textur und Farbe des Materials minimiert die Auswirkung der Renovierung. Bodenbretter aus Afromosiaholz verbinden die beiden Räume miteinander und sorgen für ein warmes Ambiente. Die Möbel in Schlafzimmer und Küche sind weiß gestrichen und harmonisieren so mit den Wänden. Die subtile Neuordnung dieses Innenraumes –warmes Material wie z.B. Holz, natürliche Stoffe für Stühle und Vorhänge und gut platzierte Farbtupfer– respektieren die Originalität des Gebäudes.

The subtle refurbishment of this interior—with warm materials such as wood and natural fabrics—retains the original character of the home.

L'agencement subtil de cet intérieur –matériaux chauds comme le bois et tissus naturels– conservent le caractère d'origine de cette maison.

Die subtile Neuordnung des Innenraumes - warmes Material wie Holz, natürliche Stoffe für Stühle und Vorhänge und gut platzierte Farbtupfer - respektieren die Originalität des Gebäudes.

Apartment in Plaza Mayor
Appartement sur la Plaza Mayor
Appartement an der Plaza Mayor

Madrid, Spain

The underlying premise of the renovation of this building in Madrid was respect for the structural elements, since it was generally in a poor condition. The architect created an orthogonal layout that reorganized the space around load-bearing walls with a significant structural function. The new distribution divides the loft into two large zones: one for the primary living space, and another, of similar dimensions, that is broken down into smaller components. The smaller area contains a studio, which was placed against a transparent glass wall with built-in shelves and a long stainless-steel work desk that looks on to the bedroom. The relationships between the spaces are established with transparent elements like glass, or simple drapes that can be used as a partition. The predominant use of pale colors provides unity and emphasizes the feeling of spaciousness.

La condition sine qua non de la restauration de cet édifice madrilène est de respecter les éléments structuraux, la construction elle-même étant en mauvais état. L'architecte a conçu un plan orthogonal qui redistribue l'espace autour de murs porteurs essentiels sur le plan structurel. La distribution actuelle divise le loft en deux grandes zones : l'une pour les espaces de vie essentiels, l'autre, aux dimensions similaires, divisée en éléments plus petits. La plus petite zone comprend un studio, placé contre un vitrage transparent doté d'étagères intégrées et d'un bureau en acier inoxydable tout en longueur qui donne sur la chambre. Les espaces sont reliés par des éléments transparents, à l'instar du verre ou de simples tentures utilisées comme cloisons. La prédominance de couleurs pales crée une unité et accentue la sensation d'espace.

Die zugrunde liegende Vorgabe der Renovierung dieses Gebäudes, das sich allgemein in einem schlechten Zustand befand, war es, die strukturellen Elemente zu respektieren. Der Architekt hat ein orthogonales Layout entworfen und den Raum um tragende Wände mit einer entscheidenden strukturellen Funktion neu organisiert. Das Loft ist jetzt in 2 Teile unterteilt: einen reinen Wohnraum und einen anderen, mit ähnlichen Abmessungen, der in kleinere Komponenten gegliedert wurde. Der kleinere Bereich enthält ein Studio in Anlehnung an eine durchsichtige Glaswand mit eingebauten Regalen und einen langen Arbeitstisch aus Edelstahl, der auf ein Schlafzimmer weist. Die Verbindung zwischen den Räumen wird durch transparente Elemente wie z.B. Glas geschaffen oder einfache Vorhänge, die als Trennwände dienen. Die vorrangige Verwendung sanfter Farben verstärkt den Eindruck von Einheit und gibt das Gefühl von Weite.

The architect created orthogonal order. He reorganized the space around load-bearing walls that have an important structural function.

L'architecte a conçu un agencement orthogonal. Il a réorganisé l'espace autour de murs porteurs importants sur le plan structural.

Der Architekt hat einen orthogonal ausgerichteten Entwurf vorgelegt. Der Raum wurde neu aufgeteilt und die Stützwände übernehmen eine wichtige strukturelle Funktion.

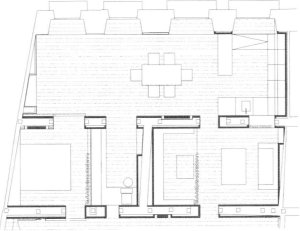

91

Loft in New York

Loft à New York

Loft in New York

New York, United States

Writer Joel Siegel and his wife, painter Ena Swansea, bought this loft to create a space where they could both live and work. The original character of the building—an early twentieth-century factory—was respected, and its vaulted ceiling, plastered walls, and industrial details were retained. The restoration work used products and materials from the period and left the electrical installations and pipes exposed. The north-facing studio allows the artist to enjoy panoramic views through the large windows. The office occupies the center of the loft and offers a space for relaxation and private entertainment as well as for writing and painting. The most private areas—the bedrooms, bathrooms, and dressing room—are situated along the perimeter of the loft, partitioned off from the other areas. The office, visually and acoustically isolated from the rest of the home, is the only room in which the wood flooring was preserved.

L'écrivain Joel Siegel et son épouse, la peintre Ena Swansea, ont acheté ce loft pour en faire un lieu de vie et de travail commun. Le caractère original de l'édifice –usine du début du XXe siècle– a été conservé, avec ses plafonds voûtés, ses murs en plâtre et les détails industriels. Le travail de restauration a utilisé des produits et matériaux d'époque, laissant les installations électriques et la tuyauterie apparentes. Le studio situé au nord permet à l'artiste de profiter des vues panoramiques par le biais de grandes fenêtres. Le bureau est placé au centre du loft. Il est aménagé d'un espace détente et loisirs réservé aussi à l'écriture et à la peinture. Les espaces plus privés du loft –chambres, salles de bains et dressing– se trouvent le long de son périmètre, séparés des autres zones. Le bureau, insonorisé et isolé sur le plan visuel du reste de l'habitation, est la seule pièce qui a conservé le parquet d'origine.

Der Schriftsteller Joel Siegel und seine Frau, die Malerin Ena Swansea, haben dieses Loft erworben, um sich einen Raum zu schaffen, in dem sie sowohl leben als auch arbeiten können. Der ursprüngliche Charakter des Gebäudes –einer Fabrik aus dem frühen 20. Jh.– wurde beibehalten und die gewölbte Decke, die vergipsten Wände und andere Details wurden integriert. Bei der Neugestaltung wurden Produkte und Material aus dieser Zeit verwendet, die elektrischen Installationen sowie die Rohre blieben sichtbar. Das nach Norden weisende Studio bietet dem Künstler einen Panoramablick durch die großen Fenster. Das Büro liegt in der Mitte des Lofts. Die privaten Bereiche –Schlafzimmer, Bäder und Ankleideräume– sind außen angebracht und von den anderen Bereichen getrennt. Das Büro, das visuell und akustisch vom restlichen Wohnbereich getrennt wurde, ist der einzige Raum, in dem der Holzboden erhalten blieb.

› Plan Plan Grundriss

The office occupies the center of the loft and offers a space for relaxation and private entertainment, as well as for writing and painting.

L'espace bureau occupe le centre du loft et offre une zone consacrée à la détente et aux occupations privées, ainsi qu'à l'écriture et à la peinture.

Das Büro liegt in der Mitte des Lofts und bietet Raum für Entspannung, aber auch zum Schreiben und Malen.

Refurbishment of a Stable
Transformation d'un étable
Umbau eines Stalles

Sant Cugat, Spain

This building originally housed a stable and later became a dressmaker's workshop. After years of vacancy and disuse, two young couples restored the space according to their housing requirements. The area that once housed the stable is now the living room, which preserves the original, vaulted Catalan herringbone ceiling. Light is the focus in the studio, thanks to a glass ceiling and a glass door that opens onto a small garden with a Japanese feel. For both the interior and the exterior space, the architects chose a wooden floor that unifies the house and gives it a feeling of length and spaciousness. Another highlight is the differentiation of two distinct atmospheres: the interior combines antique elements with simple lines, while the exterior is much more modern.

Ce bâtiment, une ancienne étable, est devenu plus tard un atelier de couturier. Laissé à l'abandon pendant de longues années, deux jeunes couples l'ont restauré selon leurs besoins personnels. Ce qui avant était l'étable abrite désormais le salon, avec son plafond catalan d'origine, voûté et à chevrons. La lumière est l'élément central du studio, grâce à un plafond en verre et une porte de la même matière qui s'ouvre sur un petit jardin à la japonaise. A l'intérieur comme à l'extérieur, les architectes ont choisi de mettre du parquet, conférant à la maison une sensation d'unité, de longueur et d'espace. Point d'orgue de la construction : la création de deux ambiances différentes avec l'intérieur mêlant antiquités et lignes épurées et l'intérieur beaucoup plus empreint de modernisme.

Dieses Gebäude war ursprünglich ein Stall und wurde später in das Atelier eines Schneiders umgebaut. Nachdem es mehrere Jahre lang leer stand, haben zwei junge Paare den Raum ausgebaut, um sich dort eigene Wohnungen einzurichten. In dem Bereich, der einst der Stall war, befindet sich jetzt das Wohnzimmer. Hier blieb die original gewölbte katalonische Fischgratdecke erhalten. Wichtigstes Element ist hier, dank des Glasdaches und einer Glastür, das Licht. Die Tür führt in einen kleinen, japanisch anmutenden Garten. Der Architekt entschied sich sowohl innen als auch außen für einen durchgängigen Holzboden, was dem Gebäude ein Gefühl von Länge und Weitläufigkeit verleiht. Ein weiteres Highlight sind die verschiedenen Stimmungen, die erzeugt werden: Im Inneren werden antike Elemente mit einfachen Linien verbunden, das Äußere wirkt sehr viel moderner.

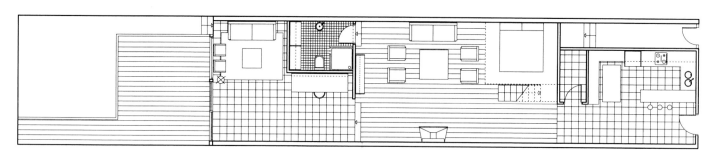

› Plan Plan Grundriss

House in Omaha
Maison à Omaha
Haus in Omaha

Omaha, United States

The architect Randy Brown decided to set up his studio-residence in a 1,725-square-foot building that was formerly a nursery school, although this had closed down in 1970. The design was based on a series of basic principles, such as the idea of living and working in the same space. The two-story building includes the studio and living areas (entrance hall, kitchen, dining room, bathroom, and office), located on the first floor, with the bedroom and dressing room on the second floor. Downstairs, the architect has marked out three areas. The studio is on one side, the dining room and conference room are in the middle, and the kitchen and bathroom are on the other. The conference room contains the most representative piece of design furniture in the home: a pine framework with laminated steel plate, the lower part of which adjoins the dining-room table and the upper part of which forms the headboard of the bed in the second-floor bedroom.

L'architecte Randy Brown a décidé d'installer son studio/résidence dans un bâtiment de 160 m², une ancienne maternelle fermée en 1970. La conception du design est partie de principes de base, dont l'idée de vivre et travailler dans le même espace. Ce bâtiment de deux étages comprend le studio et les aires de vie –hall d'entrée, cuisine, salle à manger, salle de bains et bureau–, au premier étage et au deuxième, la chambre et le dressing. En bas, l'architecte a délimité trois espaces. Le studio d'un côté, la salle à manger et salle de conférence au milieu, la cuisine et la salle de bains de l'autre. La salle de conférence possède la plus belle pièce de design de la maison : une composition structurale en pin sur un socle d'acier. La partie basse est adjacente à la salle à manger et la partie supérieure forme la tête du lit de la chambre au deuxième étage.

Der Architekt Randy Brown richtete sein Studio in diesem 160 m² großen Gebäude ein, das ehemal ein Kindergarten war, der bereits 1970 geschlossen wurde. Es war für ihn ausgesprochen wichtig, am selben Ort leben und arbeiten zu können. In dem zweigeschossigen Gebäude liegen das Studio und die Wohnbereiche (Eingangsbereich, Küche, Esszimmer, Bad und Büro) im ersten Stock und das Schlaf- und Ankleidezimmer sind im zweiten untergebracht. Unten hat der Architekt drei Bereiche abgetrennt: Das Studio befindet sich auf einer Seite, das Wohnzimmer und der Konferenzraum in der Mitte und Küche und Badezimmer auf der anderen Seite. Im Konferenzraum befindet sich das repräsentativste Designmöbeldes Hauses: Ein Rahmen aus Kiefernholz mit laminierter Stahlplatte, dessen unterer Teil den Esstisch bildet und der obere Teil zum Kopfteil des Bettes im Schlafzimmer oben gehört.

The glass façade guarantees natural light and opens up a connection with the surrounding garden.

La façade en verre de la maison fait entrer la lumière naturelle et crée un lien avec le jardin qui l'entoure.

Die Glasfassade des Hauses filtert das Tageslicht und bildet gleichzeitig eine Verbindung zum Garten.

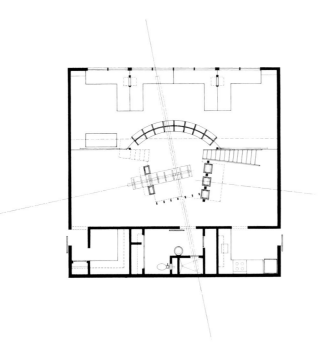

> Ground floor   Rez-de-chaussée   Erdgeschoss

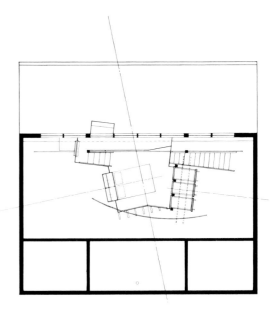

> First floor   Premier étage   Erstes Obergeschoss

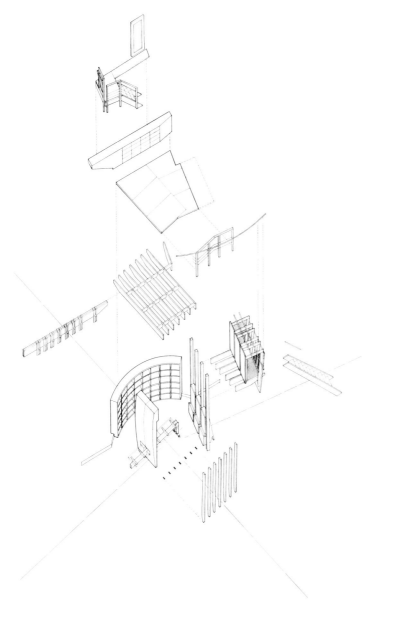

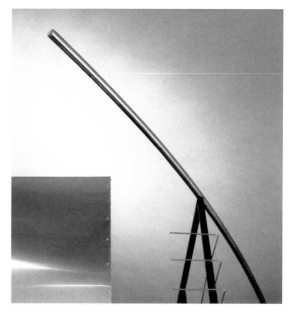

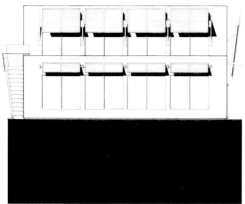

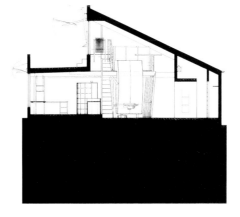

› Elevation Élévation Aufriss

› Cross section Section transversale Querschnitt

All the construction elements were designed by the architect. Some of the walls have been left bare so they can be used to exhibit his work.

Tous les éléments de la construction ont été entièrement conçus par l'architecte. Certains des murs sont entièrement nus pour qu'il puisse y exposer ses projets.

Alle Bauelemente wurden vom Architekten entworfen. Einige der Wände sind leer belassen, damit er hier seine Projekte ausstellen kann.

The bathroom and kitchen were both built with recycled materials.

La salle de bains comme la cuisine sont construites toutes les deux à base de matériaux recyclés.

Sowohl das Badezimmer als auch die Küche wurden mit wiederverwertbaren Materialien gestaltet.

Loft in London
Loft à Londres
Loft in London

London, United Kingdom

The unusual height of the ceilings of this made it possible to introduce a working area endowed with a sense of privacy but also perfectly integrated into the surrounding living area. The living room, kitchen, bedroom, and bathroom are located on the main level. The front wall is made up of small glass blocks that filter light into the entire space. In the kitchen, floor-to-ceiling closets hide the food supplies, while a panel overhead is fitted with spotlights that illuminate the work area. The focal point of this lower level is a wooden island finished with red lacquer. A mezzanine supported by a stainless steel structure and flanked by a staircase was inserted underneath the highest point of the pitched roof. This mezzanine provides an office space and is set off from all the other areas in the home.

La hauteur inhabituelle des plafonds de ce loft a permis d'installer une aire de travail dotée d'une certaine intimité tout en s'intégrant à merveille au reste de l'espace de vie. Le salon, la cuisine, la chambre et la salle de bains sont situés sur le niveau principal. La façade est constituée de petits blocs de verre qui filtre la lumière sur tout l'espace intérieur. Dans la cuisine, des armoires murales abritent les réserves et un panneau encastré au-dessus est muni de spots qui éclairent le plan de travail. Un îlot tout en bois, habillé de laque rouge, est le point de mire de ce rez-de-chaussée. Une mezzanine soutenue par une structure en acier et flanquée d'un escalier est fixée au plus haut point du toit en pinacle. Cette mezzanine, qui fait office de bureau, est séparée du reste de la maison.

Die ungewöhnliche Deckenhöhe dieses Lofts ermöglichte es, einen Arbeitsbereich zu schaffen, der zwar abgetrennt, aber dennoch in den umgebenden Wohnbereich eingebunden bleibt. Wohnzimmer, Küche, Schlafzimmer und Bad befinden sich im Hauptgeschoss. Die vordere Wand aus kleinen Glassteinen filtert Licht in den gesamten Raum. In der Küche verdecken Schränke vom Boden bis zur Decke die Vorräte, über der Arbeitsfläche sind mehrere Spots angebracht. Das Hauptaugenmerk dieser Ebene fällt auf eine Holzinsel aus rotem Lack. Ein Zwischendeck, das von einem Gerüst aus Edelstahl getragen und von einem Treppenaufgang flankiert wird, ist unter den höchsten Punkt des Daches eingefügt. Auf dem Zwischendeck befindet sich das Büro, das sich damit von den anderen Wohnbereichen abgrenzt.

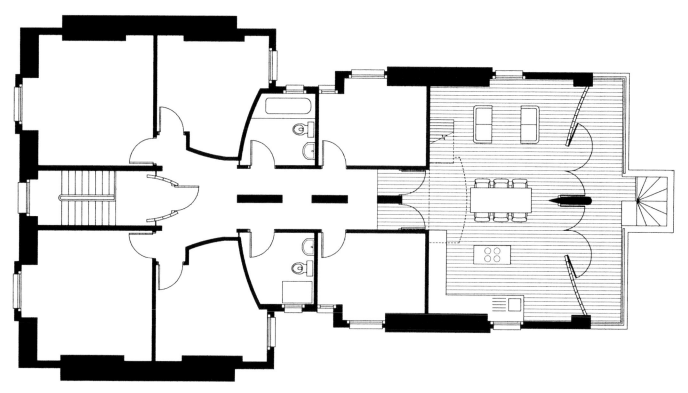

› Plan Plan Grundriss

Four-level Loft
Loft sur quatre niveaux
Vierstöckiges Loft

Barcelona, Spain

This home was refurbished by the architect Joan Bach, who designed the first stories to accommodate an apartment for his own use, with an office included. The uniqueness of the loft apartment lies in the creation of four differentiated levels that contain a space for each function without the use of walls. Apart for the bathrooms, the rooms are interconnected, at least partially. The ground floor contains the entrance, a small reception office and a bathroom. A mechanically operated metal platform provides access to the bedroom and bathroom, located above the hall. From the access floor, three steps descend to the double-height living room and to a small patio that allows abundant natural light into the apartment. The living room, with its increased height, has a attic extension, with a studio that enjoys views of the exterior.

Ce logement a été rénové par l'architecte Joan Bach qui a conçu les premiers étages pour abriter un appartement et un bureau pour son usage personnel. L'originalité de ce loft repose sur la création de quatre niveaux différents qui forment un espace pour chaque fonction en l'absence de murs. A l'exception de la salle de bains, les pièces sont reliées entre elles, tout au moins partiellement. Le rez-de-chaussée abrite l'entrée, un petit bureau de réception et une salle de bains. Une plate-forme actionnée mécaniquement permet d'accéder à la chambre à coucher et à la salle de bains, situées au-dessus du hall d'entrée. Depuis l'entrée, trois marches descendent vers le salon double hauteur et vers un petit patio permettant à la lumière d'entrer à flots dans l'appartement. Le salon, tout en hauteur, possède une extension sous les combles, dotée d'un studio avec vue sur l'extérieur.

Dieses Loft wurde vom Architekten Joan Bach neu gestaltet, der die ersten Etagen entwarf, um dort ein Appartement mit Büro für sich selbst zu schaffen. Die Einzigartigkeit des Lofts liegt in den vier verschiedenen Ebenen, die ohne Wände, Raum für jede einzelne Funktion bieten. Abgesehen von den Badezimmern sind alle Zimmer zumindest teilweise miteinander verbunden. Im Erdgeschoss befinden sich der Eingang, eine kleine Rezeption und ein Badezimmer. Eine mechanisch betriebene Plattform bietet Zugang zum Schlaf- und Badezimmer über dem Eingang. Von dieser Etage aus führen drei Stufen zum hohen Wohnzimmer und in einen kleinen Innenhof der den Einfall von natürlichem Tageslicht in das Loft ermöglicht. Das Wohnzimmer verfügt über einen Zwischenboden. Hier steht jetzt ein Studio, von dem aus man einen herrlichen Blick auf die Umgebung genießt.

The home's high ceilings, large windows and skylights create wide spaces and luminosity.

La hauteur de plafond du bâtiment, les grandes baies vitrées et les velux créent de grands espaces, baignés de lumière.

Die hohe Decke, große Fenster und Dachluken schaffen ein Gefühl von Weitläufigkeit und Helligkeit.

› Ground floor Rez-de-chaussée Erdgeschoss

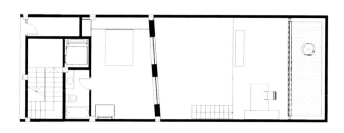

› First floor Premier étage Erstes Obergeschoss

West Village Apartment

Appartement à West Village

Appartement in West Village

New York, United States

The aim of this project was to create an interior that functioned as both a home and office for a graphic designer within a small one-bedroom apartment. A wooden structure 13 ft long and 8 ft high was created to divide the living room from the bedroom, while also allowing transit on both sides. This structure therefore functions in two modes. In the home position, it takes on the form of a box that is solid on all sides except for a deep, angled opening that offers selective views. A low, cushioned bench that serves as both a couch and guest bed is cantilevered out of the structure. In the work position, the box opens up by way of large folding panels to transform the living room into an office. The cantilevered couch automatically slides out of sight to reveal two fully fitted workstations.

Le but de ce projet est de créer un intérieur conjuguant domicile et bureau pour un designer graphiste, dans un petit studio d'une chambre. Une structure en bois 3,9 m de long et 2,4 m de large sépare le salon de la chambre à coucher, tout en laissant le passage entre les deux. Elle dispose de deux modes de fonctionnement. Dans la position logement, elle prend la forme d'une boîte d'un seul tenant à l'exception d'une ouverture d'angle profonde qui offre une série de vues. Un banc bas et recouvert de coussins sert à la fois de divan et de lit d'amis. Il est installé en porte à faux hors de la structure. Dans la position travail la boîte s'ouvre grâce à une grande cloison pliante pour transformer le salon en bureau. Le divan en cantilever disparaît automatiquement de la vue pour laisser la place à deux coins bureau entièrement équipés.

Ziel des Projektes war es, einen Raum innerhalb eines kleinen Appartements in Manhattans West Village zu schaffen, der sowohl als Wohnung als auch als Büro für einen Grafikdesigner dienen konnte. Ein Holzgerüst, 4 x 3,5 m, trennt Wohn- und Schlafzimmer. Es hat zwei Funktionen gleichzeitig: In der Position Wohnung bildet es eine Art soliden Kasten, der nur auf einer Seite geöffnet wird, um vereinzelt Einblicke zu gewähren. Eine niedrige, mit Kissen versehene Bank, die sowohl als Sofa als auch als Gästebett dient, ragt aus dem Gerüst heraus. In der Position Arbeit wird der Kasten mit großen Falttafeln geöffnet, um das Wohnzimmer in ein Büro zu verwandeln. Das Sofa gleitet automatisch weg, um den Blick freizugeben auf zwei voll ausgestattete Computer.

The box opens up by way of large folding panels to transform the living room into an office and send the cantilevered couch automatically gliding away.

L'ouverture de la boîte se fait par le biais de panneaux à double battants pour moduler le salon en un bureau. Le sofa en cantilever s'écarte automatiquement.

Der Kasten wird über große Faltwände geöffnet, um das Wohnzimmer in ein Büro zu verwandeln, wobei das herausragende Sofa dabei weggleitet.

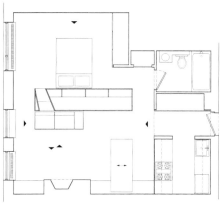

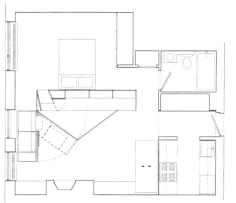

› Plans Plans Grundrisse

The table slips out for dining when the office is closed, and slides back against the wall to double as a work surface when the office is open.

Lorsque le bureau est fermé, la table se déplie pour le repas et glisse automatiquement contre le mur pour faire office de table de bureau lorsque celui-ci est à nouveau ouvert.

Der Tisch fährt zum Essen heraus wenn das Büro geschlossen ist und gleitet zurück um als Arbeitsfläche zu dienen wenn das Büro geöffnet ist.

Wedding Loft

Three people share this 3,300 square foot loft as a home and workspace. The old factory, dating from the 1920s, was refurbished in 1998, with the aim of preserving the industrial character of the building as far as possible. Three bedrooms, separate from the common living space, provide an intimate retreat for each of the inhabitants. The industrial elevator, which has been retained, leads directly to the entrance of the loft but the door can only be opened with a key. There, the main room is located where everyone of the young creatives placed its own little working zone, consisting of a computer desk, a music studio and a regular desk top. Behind a curved wall, a more private office is located, which serves for work which has to be done in calm. The bathroom involves a degree of inconvenience as it is in the corridor, and is for communal use, but this is compensated by the advantages of this extraordinary space.

Trois personnes partagent ce loft de 300 m², réunissant à la fois habitation et bureau. L'ancienne usine, datant des années 20, a été restaurée en 1998, en gardant tant que possible le cachet industriel du bâtiment. Trois chambres à coucher, séparées de l'espace de vie commun, constituent la sphère privée où chacun des occupants peut se retirer. L'ascenseur industriel, qui a été conservé, mène directement à l'entrée du loft dont la porte ne s'ouvre qu'avec une clé. Ici, la pièce principale est la zone ou chacun de ces jeunes créateurs installe sa propre sphère de travail, composée d'un ordinateur, d'un studio de musique et d'un bureau normal. Un mur tout en courbes masque un bureau plus privé, propice au travail qui requiert le calme. L'emplacement de la salle de bains commune n'est pas idéal. Mais cet inconvénient est compensé par les avantages qu'offre cet espace extraordinaire.

Dieses knapp 300 m² große Loft nutzen drei Bewohner sowohl als Wohnraum und Arbeitsplatz. Die alte Fabrik aus den 20er Jahren wurde 1998 von Grund auf renoviert. Dabei wollte man so weit als möglich den gewerblichen Charakter des Gebäudes erhalten. Drei große Schlafzimmer bieten jedem Bewohner einen eigenen Privatraum, in den er sich zurückziehen kann. Ein alter Industrieaufzug führt direkt in das Loft, kann aber nur mit einem Schlüssel geöffnet werden. Hier befindet sich der Hauptraum, in dem jeder der jungen Kreativen seinen eigenen Arbeitsplatz eingerichtet hat. Hinter einer gebogenen Wand befindet sich ein privates Büro, das als ruhigeres Arbeitszimmer genutzt wird. Das Badezimmer befindet sich im Flur und wird von allen genutzt, doch diese Nachteile werden durch die Außergewöhnlichkeit des restlichen Gebäudes mehr als kompensiert.

A open plan distribution and a large amount of light, creating a bright, post-modern atmosphere.

Une distribution ouverte de l'espace et une luminosité extraordinaire, engendre une atmosphère post-moderne éblouissante de clarté.

Eine offene Verteilung des Raumes und viel Licht schaffen ein helles, postmodernes Ambiente.

Behind a curved wall, a more private office is located which serves for work which has to be done in calm.

Un mur tout en courbes masque un bureau plus privé, davantage propice au travail qui doit se faire dans le calme.

Hinter einer gekrümmten Wand befindet sich ein privates Büro, das als ruhigeres Arbeitszimmer genutzt wird.

Loft in Abbot Kinney
Loft d'Abbot Kinney
Loft in Abbot Kinney

Venice, United States

An ever-growing number of designers, multimedia companies, and artists are choosing the Abbot Kinney neighborhood as their base. These professionals are not only looking for a neighborhood in tune with lifestyle, but also for interior spaces that adapt to their requirements. They are searching for more casual, informal, and flexible environments that allow them to live and work in the same space. This project consists of a typical adaptation of the traditional artist's loft, with large, open spaces that can be used for living or working, as required. The layout includes three different lofts that share the same structure, materials, and color scheme, giving it the appearance of a compact building. These characteristics permitted the creation of a continuous façade and a row of stores looking on to the street. All the units are separated by patios and are equipped with balconies, terraces, and glassed-in areas.

De plus en plus de designers, compagnies de multimédia et d'artistes choisissent de s'installer dans les environs de Abbot Kinney. Ils ne sont pas uniquement en quête d'un environnement adapté à leur style de vie, mais aussi d'espaces intérieurs correspondant à leurs exigences. Ces professionnels recherchent un cadre de vie plus décontracté, informel et flexible leur permettant de travailler et vivre dans le même espace. Ce projet est un cas de rénovation de loft traditionnel d'artiste : grands espaces ouverts modulables pour y vivre ou y travailler. Le plan comprend trois lofts différents mais unis par une structure, des matériaux et une palette de couleurs similaires, sous l'aspect d'un édifice compact. Tout cela a conduit à la création d'une façade continue et d'une rangée de magasins donnant sur la rue. Toutes ces unités sont séparées par des patios et dotées de balcons, terrasses et vérandas.

Immer mehr Designer, Multimedia-Unternehmen und Künstler wählen den Stadtteil von Abbot Kinney als Heimat. Sie suchen dabei nicht nur ein Stadtviertel, das ihrem Lifestyle entspricht, sondern auch Wohnbereiche, die ihren Anforderungen gerecht werden. Eine entspannte, informelle und flexible Umgebung, die es ihnen ermöglicht, im selben Raum zu leben und zu arbeiten. Das Projekt besteht aus einer typischen Adaption des traditionellen Künstlerlofts mit großen, offenen Flächen. Der Grundriss umfasst drei nebeneinander liegende Lofts, die alle dieselbe Struktur, dasselbe Material und Farbschema aufweisen und dadurch den Eindruck eines kompakten Gebäudes vermitteln. Diese Merkmale ermöglichten den Bau einer durchgängigen Fassade und einer Reihe von Läden, die zur Straße weisen. Alle Einheiten sind durch Innenhöfe voneinander getrennt und mit Balkonen, Terrassen und verglasten Bereichen ausgestattet.

All the areas in the loft are separated by patios and equipped with balconies, terraces, and glassed-in areas.

Toutes les zones du loft sont séparées par des patios et sont dotées de balcons, terrasses et vérandas.

Alle Einheiten sind durch Innenhöfe voneinander getrennt und mit Balkonen, Terrassen und verglasten Bereichen ausgestattet.

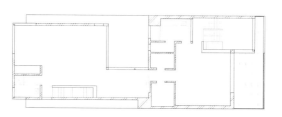

› **Ground floor** Rez-de-chaussée Erdgeschoss

› **First floor** Premier étage Erstes Obergeschoss

› **Second floor** Deuxième étage Zweites Obergeschoss

Dwelling and Showroom

Habitation et salle d'exposition

Haus und Ausstellungsraum

New York, United States

This loft was remodelated to accommodate a home and an art exhibition area. Since the client, a art collector, wanted these two functions to coexist without any strict distinctions, the architects developed a design that merges the gallery with the private spaces. The lower floor of the duplex space houses the master bedroom, living room, dining room, kitchen, projection room, painting studio, storeroom, and large terrace. The upper floor contains two sub-levels: one for the guest rooms and the other for a studio. These work areas did not exist in the original configuration, but the designers took advantage of the height of the ceilings to install them, using reinforced concrete, and lining their edges with guard rails of black-painted steel or tempered glass. The same concrete was also used on the upper floor in some columns and facings.

Ce loft a été rehabilité pour y installer un logement et une aire d'exposition d'œuvres d'art. Le client, collectionneur d'art, ne désirait pas de stricte séparation entre ces deux fonctions. Les architectes ont donc conçu un plan où galerie et espaces privés se fondent. L'étage inférieur du duplex abrite la chambre à coucher du maître des lieux, le salon, la salle à manger, la cuisine, la salle de projection, le studio de peinture, le débarras et une grande terrasse. L'étage supérieur est divisé en deux sous-niveaux : un pour les chambres d'amis et l'autre pour le studio. Ces espaces de travail n'étaient pas prévus dans la configuration initiale, mais le designer a tiré parti de la hauteur du plafond pour les installer en utilisant du béton armé, doublé en bordure de rails de garde en acier noir ou en verre trempé. Un béton identique a été utilisé à l'étage supérieur pour certaines colonnes et quelques revêtements.

Dieses Loft wurde neu gestaltet und darin sowohl eine Wohnung als auch einen Ausstellungsbereich geschaffen. Da der Kunde, ein Kunstsammler, diese beiden Funktionen nebeneinander ohne klare Abgrenzungen verwirklicht sehen wollte, entwarfen die Architekten einen Plan, bei dem die Galerie mit privaten Räumen vereint wird. In der unteren Etage des Zweifamilienhauses befinden sich Schlaf-, Wohn-, Esszimmer, Küche, Projektionsraum, Malatelier, Lagerraum und eine große Terrasse. Oben gibt es zwei Ebenen: eine für die Gästezimmer und eine weitere für ein Studio. Diese Arbeitsbereiche waren im ursprünglichen Entwurf nicht vorgesehen, aber die Designer wollten die Höhe der Decken ausnutzen. Die Ecken der Betonstützpfeiler sind mit schwarz bemaltem Stahl oder geschwärztem Glas verstärkt. Derselbe Beton wurde auf der oberen Etage an einigen Säulen und Verkleidungen verwendet.

The height of the ceilings allowed to subdivide the work areas on two sub-levels.

La hauteur du plafond permettait de subdiviser les aires de travail sur deux sous niveaux.

Der Designer hat die Höhe der Decken mit einbezogen und Arbeitsbereiche auf zwei Ebenen geschaffen.

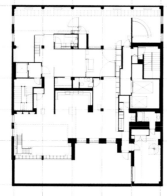

› Ground floor Rez-de-chaussée Erdgeschoss

› First floor Premier étage Erstes Obergeschoss

House in Portola Valley
Maison à Portola Valley
Haus im Portola Valley

Portola Valley, United States

The architects assigned for this project had to come up with a design that would fit in with the pre-existing environment of this neighborhood, while also embodying contemporary ideals. The clients, for their part, wanted a home that would incorporate attractive workspaces. The design of the house, therefore, had to focus on both the public areas and those used for business meetings. The architects' response to these requirements was to set the public spaces on the lower level and the private spaces on the upper floor, facing in the opposite direction from those of the lower level to enjoy the view of the valley. The composition is based on a series of long, brightly colored walls that extend across the lot, with a few transversal planes that create a series of rooms to fulfill the requirements of the internal functions.

Les architectes chargés de ce projet ont dû concevoir une construction en harmonie avec la proximité de cette localité préexistante, tout en incarnant les critères d'architecture contemporaine. Les clients, eux, désiraient un logement intégrant des espaces de travail agréables. Le design de la maison devait donc se centrer à la fois sur les zones publiques et sur celles consacrées aux réunions d'affaires. En réponse à ces contraintes, les architectes ont installé les espaces publics au niveau inférieur et les sphères privées à l'étage supérieur, à l'opposé des zones de l'étage inférieur, pour bénéficier de la vue sur la vallée. La composition architecturale comprend une série de longs murs, hauts en couleurs qui s'étirent au travers du terrain, coupés par quelques plans transversaux qui créent une série de pièces pour répondre aux fonctions internes requises.

Die Architekten dieses Projektes mussten einen Entwurf vorlegen, der den Bau in das bestehende Wohnviertel aus den 50er Jahren einfügt und gleichzeitig modernen Vorstellungen entspricht. Die Kunden wünschten sich ein Heim mit einem schönen Arbeitsplatz. Der Entwurf des Hauses musste sich also sowohl auf die öffentlich zugänglichen Bereiche, als auch auf die konzentrieren, die für geschäftliche Treffen vorgesehen waren. Die öffentlichen Bereiche wurden auf die untere Ebene verteilt, die privaten nach oben. Die obere Etage weist in die entgegen gesetzte Richtung, um den Blick auf das Tal zu ermöglichen. Das Gebäude besteht aus einer Reihe von langen, farbenfrohen Wänden mit wenigen transversalen Flächen, die eine Reihe von Zimmern bilden.

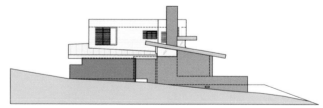

› Elevations Élévations Aufrisse

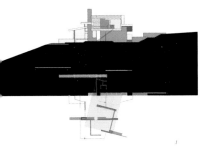
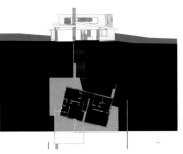

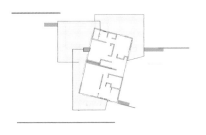

› **Sections** Sections Schnitte

› **Ground floor** Rez-de-chaussée Erdgeschoss

› **First floor** Premier étage Erstes Obergeschoss

The combination of wooden floors and red-painted walls creates a warm and modern atmosphere.

L'alliance des parquets et des murs peints en rouge crée une ambiance chaleureuse et moderne.

Die Kombination von Holzböden und rot bemalten Wänden schaffen ein warmes und modern anmutendes Ambiente.

Residential Complex
Complexe résidentiel
Wohneinheit

Venice, United States

This project called for a building with six homes, with space set aside for workshops and offices. One of the premises was that the construction should blend harmoniously with its setting. So, the architects opted for an industrial design reminiscent of the area's old warehouses, with a structure made of concrete blocks and a vaulted roof. Certain elements in the interior design, such as the large sliding doors or the metal used in some of the finishing, also suggest the decor typical of a factory. The layout is divided into three parts, each of which is divided in turn by walls of concrete blocks that define the six homes and their respective workshops, with bedrooms and bathrooms on the first floor. Great spatial flexibility was required in order to simultaneously combine different activities without excessively compartmentalizing the space.

Ce projet concerne un édifice de six logements et d'ateliers et bureaux adjacents. L'une des premières contraintes étant d'harmoniser la construction à l'environnement, les architectes ont donc opté pour un design industriel inspiré des anciens entrepôts de la région, basé sur une structure alliant blocs de béton et toit voûté. Certains éléments du design d'intérieur, à l'instar des portes coulissantes ou du métal utilisé pour les détails de finition, ne sont pas sans rappeler le décor typique d'une usine. Le plan est divisé en trois parties, tour à tour séparées par des murs de blocs de béton définissant les six logements et leurs ateliers respectifs. Chambres à coucher et salles de bains sont au premier étage. Une grande flexibilité spatiale est indispensable pour combiner simultanément les diverses activités sans trop cloisonner l'espace.

Dieses Projekt umfasst sechs Wohnungen mit Ateliers und Büros. Voraussetzung war den Bau möglichst nahtlos in die Umgebung einfügen. Die Architekten haben sich für ein eher gewerbliches Design entschieden, eine nostalgische Erinnerung an die alten Lagerhäuser dieser Gegend. Die Struktur wird von Betonblöcken gebildet, das Dach ist gewölbt. Verschiedene Elemente, wie z.B. die großen Schiebetüren oder das Metall, das für die Details verwendet wurde, erinnern ebenfalls an die typische Ausstattung einer Fabrik. Der Grundriss ist in drei Teile unterteilt. Jeder davon wird wieder von Betonwänden unterbrochen, die dann sechs Wohnungen mit entsprechenden Ateliers bilden, jede Einheit davon mit Schlafzimmern und Bädern auf der ersten Etage. Eine hohe Flexibilität in Bezug auf den Raum war erforderlich, um mehreren Aktivitäten gleichzeitig zu entsprechen, ohne den Raum an sich unbedingt zu sehr unterteilen zu müssen.

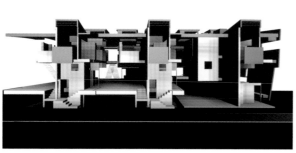
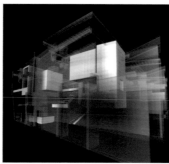

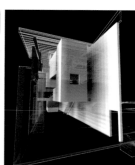

Multifunctional Attic
Attique polyvalent
Multifunktionelles Dachgeschoss

Barcelona, Spain

The refurbishment carried out in this studio sought to preserve the authenticity of its attic setting. The renovation involved remodeling an empty, almost square space with an extremely high ceiling, 12 ft at the lowest point. Due to the characteristics of the space and the activity for which it was intended—a graphic design studio—, separate workrooms were not needed. It was decided from the beginning to create different zones without visually breaking up the space. This means that the reception area and meeting room both look out on to the remaining space. In front of the reception area, an L-shape divider creates an area that is used as a meeting room. The work area is defined by a large central worktop (comprising three tables) free of any IT equipment, and a custom-designed side table that holds the computer hardware. The entire office is lit by the sunshine that entires through the glass wall facing the terrace and the large skylights.

La rénovation réalisée dans ce studio a tenté de préserver l'authenticité de cet espace sous les combles. Il s'agissait de remodeler un espace de vie, presque carré doté d'une immense hauteur de plafond, 3,5 m au point le plus bas. Les caractéristiques de l'espace et l'activité prévue entre ces murs – un studio de graphisme et design – ont permis d'éviter de faire des pièces de bureaux séparées. Dès le départ, différentes zones sont créées sans diviser l'espace sur le plan visuel : l'aire de réception et la salle de réunion s'ouvrent toutes les deux sur l'espace restant. Face à l'aire de réception, une cloison en L crée une zone utilisée comme salle de réunion. L'espace bureau est définit par un grand bloc central de travail (comprenant trois tables), sans équipement IT et une table d'appoint faite sur mesure pour le matériel d'ordinateur. La lumière du soleil inonde tout le bureau grâce aux baies vitrées face à la terrasse et aux immenses velux.

Die Modernisierung dieses Studios sollte vor allem die Authentizität des Dachgeschosses respektieren. Dabei wurde ein leerer, fast quadratischer Raum mit einem extrem hohen Dach, 3,5 m am niedrigsten Punkt, von Grund auf renoviert. Durch die charakteristischen Merkmale des Raumes und den Zweck, dem er dienen sollte, ein Studio für Grafikdesign, war es nicht erforderlich, getrennte Arbeitszimmer einzurichten. Dabei sollten aber von Anfang an unterschiedliche Bereiche innerhalb desselben Raums gebildet werden. Eine Trennwand in L-Form vor dem Empfangsbereich dient als Abgrenzung zum Konferenzraum. Den Arbeitsbereich bildet eine große, zentrale Arbeitsplatte, aus drei Tischen zusammengesetzt. Die Computer stehen auf einem maßgeschneiderten Seitentisch. Das gesamte Büro wird vom Tageslicht erhellt, das durch die Glaswand vor der Terrasse und durch die großen Dachfenster einfällt.

It was decided to create zones without visually breaking up the space, thereby allowing the rest of the area to be seen from the reception zone and the meeting room.

Il a été décidé d'emblée de créer des zones sans rupture spatiale visuelle permettant de voir le reste de l'espace depuis la zone de réception et de la salle de réunion.

Man beschloss, einzelne Bereiche zu schaffen, ohne den Raum zu unterbrechen. Dadurch kann der restliche Bereich von Rezeption und Konferenzraum aus eingesehen werden.

The main objectives were to direct natural light into the space, endow the setting with functionality and achieve a balanced, modern look.

Les objectifs de diriger la lumière dans l'espace conférant ainsi à l'environnement la fonctionnalité qui lui faisait défaut pour aboutir à un sens d'harmonie et de modernité.

Hauptziel war, Tageslicht in den Raum einfallen zu lassen, um der Umgebung eine Funktionalität zu verleihen und gleichzeitig ein ausgewogenes, modernes Ambiente zu schaffen.

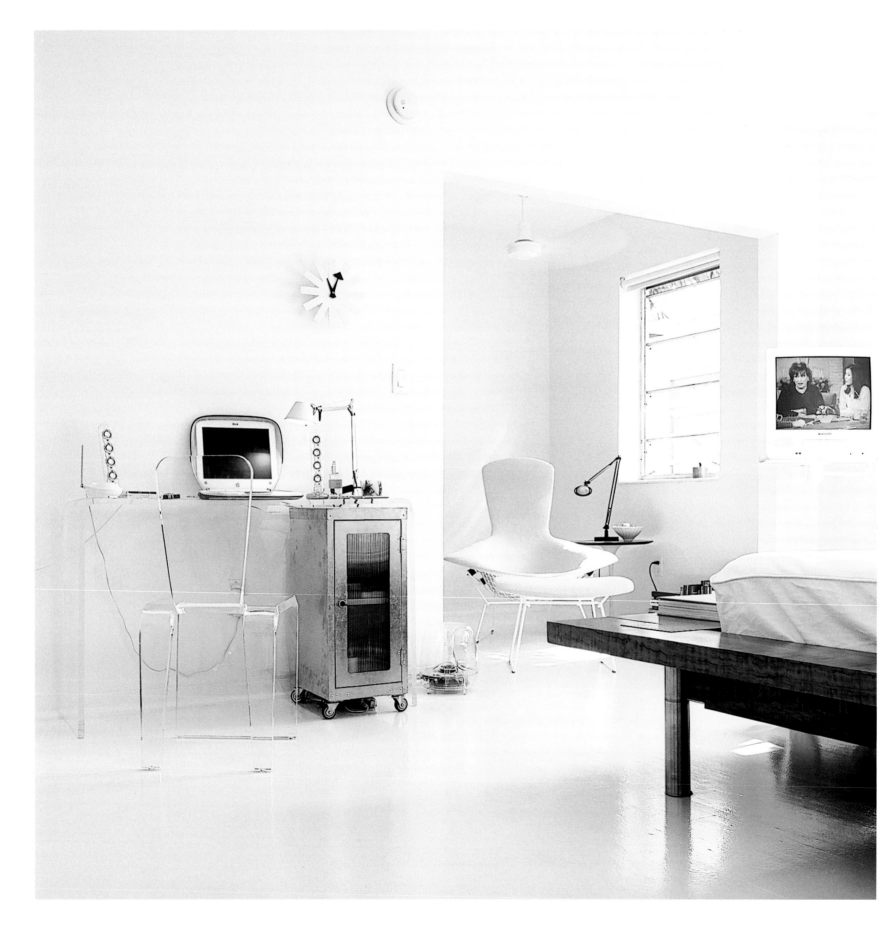

Miami, United States

Studio in Miami Beach
Studio a Miami Beach
Studio in Miami Beach

This small studio, situated on the second floor of a 1951 building, belongs to the architect who designed it. The space consists of a bedroom, bathroom, kitchen, and studio.All of the areas except the bathroom, which is reached by a corridor, are integrated into a single space. Several architectural elements, such as the aluminum windows, were restored to enhance the 1950s feel. The original wooden floor was painted white to create a contemporary atmosphere and increase the feeling of spaciousness. The furniture was chosen to make the most of the limited space and create a series of multifunctional areas. The small workspace positioned just in front of the partition includes a narrow desk, drawer unit, and a chair made of clear plastic that is barely visible to the eye. Several areas are multipurpose: a reading corner is tucked into the kitchen, and the dining area is incorporated into the living room.

Ce petit studio, situé au deuxième étage d'un édifice de 1951, est conçu par son propriétaire, architecte. L'espace se compose d'une chambre à coucher, d'une salle de bains, d'une cuisine et d'un studio. Toutes les zones, à l'exception de la salle de bains que l'on atteint par un couloir, sont intégrées en un seul espace. Certains éléments architecturaux, comme les fenêtres d'aluminium, ont été restaurés pour accentuer l'atmosphère des années 50. Le sol en bois d'origine est peint en blanc pour créer une ambiance contemporaine et accroître l'impression d'espace. Le choix des meubles permet d'optimiser l'espace limité et de créer une série de zones polyvalentes. Le petit espace de travail, placé juste devant la cloison, comprend un bureau étroit, des tiroirs et une chaise en plastique transparent à peine visible à l'œil nu. Plusieurs espaces sont polyvalents : la cuisine abrite un coin lecture et la salle à manger est intégrée au salon.

Dieses kleine Studio in der 2. Etage eines Gebäudes von 1951 gehört dem Architekten, der es auch selbst entworfen hat. Die Wohnung besteht aus einem Schlafzimmer, einem Bad, Küche und dem Studio. Verschiedene architektonische Elemente, wie z.B. die Aluminiumfenster, wurden renoviert, um das Ambiente der 50er Jahre zu erhalten. Der Originalholzboden wurde weiß gestrichen, um einen modernen Touch hinzuzufügen und das Gefühl von Weite zu unterstreichen. Die Möbel wurden im Hinblick auf den begrenzten Platz ausgewählt und um eine Reihe multifunktionaler Bereichen zu schaffen. Der kleine Arbeitsplatz direkt vor der Trennwand besteht aus einem kleinen Tisch, einem Schubkasten und einem Stuhl aus durchsichtigem Plastik, der kaum wahrnehmbar ist. Verschiedene Bereiche dienen mehreren Zwecken gleichzeitig: ein Leseplatz wurde in der Küche eingerichtet und der Essbereich befindet sich im Wohnzimmer.

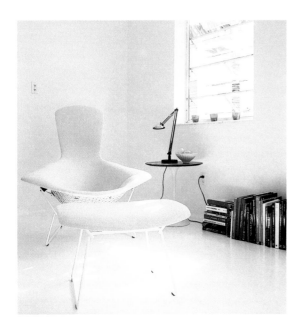

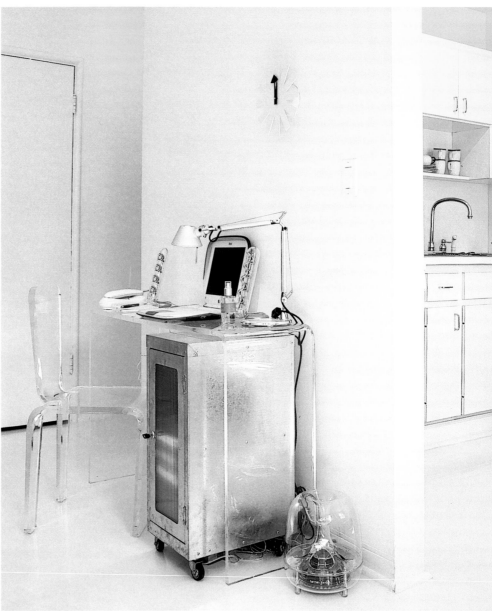

The large couch-bed dominates the space; it is situated in the center of the apartment, in an area with few other elements to detract attention from it.

Le grand lit divan domine l'espace et trône au centre de l'appartement, entouré de quelques éléments qui le mettent en valeur.

Das große Schlafsofa dominiert den Raum und steht in der Mitte des Appartements. Nur wenige andere Elemente lenken den Blick ab.

Dwelling in Buenos Aires
Maison à Buenos Aires
Haus in Buenos Aires

Buenos Aires, Argentina

Volume, space, and natural light were the functional requirements that had to be satisfied to make this home serve as a place to both live and work. The space was divided, not by structural walls or tall partitions but by a half-height, 5-ft module that serves two functions: the side facing the bed holds aluminum shelves for the entertainment equipment, while the other side is a library that incorporates two extendable light fixtures over the antique desk. Such a double-purpose partition facilitates the division between work and home, in both small and large open-plan spaces. The careful balance between modern and antique includes an eighteenth-century Austrian chest of drawers, a pair of Louis XV chairs, and a black leather chaise longue designed by Le Corbusier. The colors used, mainly white, turquoise, and black, optimize the flow of light and the overall feeling of continuity and calm.

Volume, espace et lumière naturelle sont les critères à respecter pour faire de cet espace à la fois un lieu de travail et d'habitation. La division de l'espace ne se présente pas sous forme de murs structurels ou de cloisons élevées mais par un module à mi-hauteur de 1,5 m qui a une double fonction : le côté face au lit est doté d'étagères d'aluminium pour les appareils audiovisuels et l'autre côté, est une bibliothèque avec deux points d'éclairage extensibles intégrés pour éclairer le bureau ancien. Ce genre de double cloison facilite la séparation entre le travail et la maison que ce soit dans des petits ou de grands espaces. Un subtil équilibre entre contemporain et ancien présente une commode autrichienne du XVIIIe siècle, deux chaises Louis XV et une chaise longue en cuir noir dessinée par Le Corbusier. Les couleurs employées, surtout le banc, le turquoise et le noir, optimisent le flux de lumière et la sensation omniprésente de continuité et de calme.

Volumen, Raum und Tageslicht waren die funktionellen Voraussetzungen, die erfüllt werden mussten, um dieses Haus sowohl als Wohnraum als auch als Arbeitsplatz zu nutzen. Der Raum wurde geteilt und zwar nicht durch stützenden oder hohe Trennwände, sondern durch ein 1,5 m hohes Modul, das 2 Funktionen gleichzeitig dient: die zum Bett weisende Seite verfügt über Aluminiumregale für die Unterhaltungselektronik, während die andere Seite ein Bücherregal mit zwei ausziehbaren Lampen über einem antiken Tisch darstellt. Solch ein Raumteiler ermöglicht die Trennung zwischen Arbeits- und Wohnbereich. Zu den sorgfältig ausgewählten modernen und antiken Möbeln gehören ein österreichischer Sekretär aus dem 18. Jh., zwei Louis XV-Stühle und eine schwarze Leder-Chaiselongue von Le Corbusier. Die verwendeten Farben, hauptsächlich Weiß, Türkis und Schwarz, optimieren den Einfall von Licht und den allgemeinen Eindruck von Kontinuität und Ruhe.

The colors used, mainly white, turquoise, and black, optimize the fluidity of light and the overall feeling of continuity and calm.

Les couleurs employées, surtout le blanc, le turquoise et le noir, optimisent la fluidité de la lumière et la sensation omniprésente de continuité et de calme.

Die verwendeten Farben, hauptsächlich Weiß, Türkis und Schwarz, optimieren den Einfall von Licht und den allgemeinen Eindruck von Kontinuität und Ruhe.

Office in a Garret
Bureau dans un grenier
Büro auf einem Dachboden

Prato, Italy

Carla Guerrini's studio is to be found inside a 1930's three floor semi-detached villa. This is reflected in the building decor and details and marked characteristics from that construction period and uses the first two floors as living space. The project wanted to conserve the parts most relevant to the original design but associating it nevertheless as a modern and minimalist design and reusing the top floor which previously had been used as a garret. The modern elements serve as a dividing line between the two souls of the house and are, even in their simplicity, intentionally evident. Special importance is placed on the iron elements and the use of light and perspective as an fundamental of dialogue between the dimensions. With this purpose, the project has preserved the height of the hollow of the stairs particularly for the views that can be enjoyed from that position.

Le studio de Carla Guerrini se situe au troisième étage d'une villa mitoyenne de 1930, époque qui se reflète dans les décorations et détails de l'édifice. L'espace de vie est réparti sur les deux étages. Le projet part de l'idée de conserver les éléments les plus importants du design original, tout en y ajoutant des éléments modernes et minimalistes et de réutiliser le dernier étage faisant auparavant office de grenier. Dans ce projet, les éléments modernes, d'une grande sobriété, sont sciemment mis en relief et servent à séparer les deux âmes de la maison. Une importance toute particulière est accordée aux éléments en fer et au recours à la lumière en tant que dialogue essentiel entre les différents niveaux. Dans cet esprit, le projet a conservé la hauteur de l'escalier pour savourer les différentes vues possibles à ce niveau.

Das Studio von Carla Guerrini befindet sich in einer dreistöckigen Doppelhausvilla aus den 30er Jahren. Dies wird durch die Dekoration und Details aus dieser Epoche reflektiert. Die ersten beiden Stockwerke des Gebäudes werden als Wohnraum genutzt. Bei dem Projekt sollten die wichtigsten Merkmale des Originaldesigns erhalten bleiben und dennoch ein modernes und minimalistisches Ambiente geschaffen werden. Dabei wurde dem oberen Stockwerk, das vorher als Dachboden diente, eine neue Funktion zugewiesen. Die modernen Elemente fungieren als optische Trennung zwischen den beiden Bestimmungen des Hauses. Eine besondere Bedeutung kommt den eisernen Elementen und der Verwendung von Licht und Perspektive als Grundlage eines Dialogs zwischen den Dimensionen zu. Zu diesem Zweck wurde die Höhe des Treppenhauses genutzt, um besonders schöne Ausblicke zu erlauben.

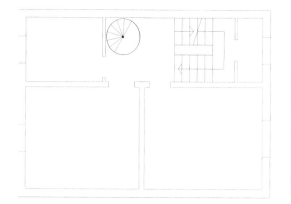

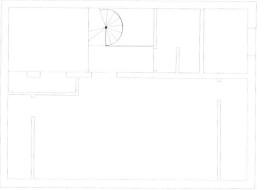

› Plan   Plan   Grundriss

Loft with Courtyard
Loft avec jardin intérieur
Ein Loft mit Innenhof

Barcelona, Spain

Antoni Casadesús has remodelled the premises formerly occupied by a textile firm and has converted it into a space capable of holding both his interior design studio and his private living space. A central strip with a small garden and the kitchen separates the most private area of the loft—the bedroom, bathroom, and attic—from a large space on two floors which opens onto the rear patio-garden. This layout allows separation of the different functions and different degrees of privacy, while at the same time maintaining a visual connection between all points of the loft. From the entrance, both the intermediate garden and the rear terrace can be seen. In spite of the considerable depth of the premises, natural light is present everywhere. Almost all the surfaces, including the floor and some pieces of furniture—a sofa, shelves, piano, and table—are either white or in pale shades.

Antoni Casadesús a remodelé le site occupé auparavant par une entreprise textile et l'a converti en un espace à même d'accueillir à la fois son studio de design d'intérieur et sa sphère privée. Une bande centrale dotée d'un petit jardin et la cuisine séparent la plus grande partie privée du loft –chambre à coucher, salle de bains et attique– d'un grand espace articulé sur deux étages et qui s'ouvre sur le patio-jardin à l'arrière du bâtiment. Cette conception spatiale permet de séparer les différentes fonctions et les différents niveaux d'intimité, tout en maintenant une relation visuelle entre tous les axes du loft. Depuis l'entrée, la vue embrasse à la fois le jardin intermédiaire et la terrasse à l'arrière. Malgré la grande profondeur des lieux, la lumière naturelle est omniprésente. Toutes les surfaces, ou presque, y compris le sol et certains meubles –divan, étagères, piano et table– s'affichent en blanc ou en teintes pâles.

Antoni Casadesús hat dieses Gebäude renoviert, in dem vorher ein Textilunternehmen untergebracht war und hat es in einen Raum verwandelt, in dem heute sowohl sein Studio für Innendesign als auch seine Privatwohnung Platz finden. Ein kleiner Garten und die Küche trennen die privaten Bereiche des Lofts, das Schlafzimmer, Bad und einen Dachboden, von einem großen Raum mit zwei Ebenen, der auf den hinteren Innenhof weist. Dieser Grundriss ermöglicht eine Abgrenzung der einzelnen Funktionen, während gleichzeitig eine visuelle Verbindung zwischen allen Räumen des Lofts erhalten bleibt. Vom Eingang aus kann man sowohl auf den kleinen Innengarten als auch auf die hintere Terrasse blicken. Trotz der verhältnismäßig großen Tiefe des Lofts fällt überall natürliches Tageslicht ein. Fast alle Oberflächen, darunter auch der Boden und einige Möbelstücke, ein Sofa, Regale, das Piano und ein Tisch, sind entweder in Weiß oder hellen Tönen gehalten.

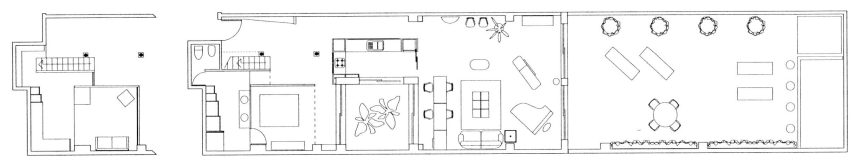

First floor Premier étage Erstes Obergeschoss   › Ground floor Rez-de-chaussée Erdgeschoss

173

Attic in Bilbao
Attique à Bilbao
Dachgeschoss in Bilbao

Bilbao, Spain

This loft is situated inside an eighteenth-century building in the old quarter of the city, and exhibits the scars of many renovations and years of wear and tear. The existing framework was maintained, eliminating any unnecessary divisions in order to facilitate the entrance of light and the distribution of space. An indirect lighting system creates the impression that the structure is levitating from the ground, reducing any perception of heaviness. The architects introduced a container to administer all the services needed in a home: kitchen, bathroom, and storage. The bathroom is easily accessed from the bedroom or the living room, as is the storage space located on one side of the container. An exposed brick wall in a corner of the living room accomodates a mixing table.

Le loft, situé dans un bâtiment du XVIIIe siècle du vieux quartier de la cité, porte les cicatrices de nombreuses restaurations et les marques du temps. La structure existante a été preservée. Les cloisons inutiles ont été éliminées afin de faciliter à la fois l'entrée de la lumière et la distribution de l'espace. Un système d'éclairage indirect crée l'impression que la structure s'élève du sol, éliminant toute sensation de lourdeur. Les architectes ont intégré un container pour tous les services domestiques : cuisine, salle de bains et stockage. Il est facile d'accéder à la salle de bains par la chambre à coucher ou le salon, comme à l'espace rangement, disposé de l'autre côté du container. Un ensemble de briques sert de superbe toile de fond à une table de mixage.

Dieses Loft befindet sich in einem Gebäude aus dem 18. Jh. in der Altstadt und wurde im Laufe der Jahre mehrmals renoviert. Das bestehende Rahmenwerk aus Holzbalken und Säulen wurde beibehalten, dabei aber alle unnötigen Trennungen entfernt, um den Lichteinfall zu ermöglichen und den Raum zu erweitern. Ein indirektes Beleuchtungssystem scheint die Struktur vom Boden abzuheben und nimmt ihr so den Eindruck von Schwere. In einem von den Architekten eingebauten Container wurden alle Servicebereiche untergebracht: Küche, Badezimmer und Lagerraum. Das Badezimmer erreicht man durch das Schlaf- oder das Wohnzimmer, den Lagerraum über eine Seite des Containers. In einer Ecke des Wohnzimmers, dient eine kleine Ziegelwand als Abgrenzung eines Bereiches für technisches Audiozubehör.

The existing framework of wood beams and structural columns was maintained, eliminating unnecessary divisions to facilitate the entry of light and the distribution of space.

La structure en poutres de bois existante et les colonnes porteuses ont été preservées. Les cloisons inutiles ont été éliminées afin de faciliter l'entrée de la lumière.

Das bestehende Rahmenwerk aus Holzbalken und Säulen wurde beibehalten, aber alle unnötigen Trennungen entfernt, um den Lichteinfall zu ermöglichen und den Raum zu erweitern.

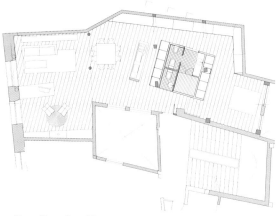

› Plan   Plan   Grundriss

A Library at Home
Une bibliothèque à domicile
Eine Bibliothek im eigenen Heim

Berlin, Germany

This dwelling is located in the city center and is characterized by its high ceilings, the original parquet floor and huge windows—all typical for residences in this area. There are five rooms given over to the almost 40.000 books in this home, so the only way for the resident to find enough space to store so many books and also have a living area for himself was by joining up two apartments. The immense stock of books is stored in huge bookcases, some of them built by the resident himself. Some art books lie exposed on the tables, while original paintings decorate the whole apartment and invite to little exhibitions. The fresco adorning the ceiling of the main library is by the English artist Burt Irvin. Modern technology is not welcome here and visitors will search in vain for a television or radio.

Cette demeure, située au centre de la cité, se définit par ses hauts plafonds, le parquet d'origine et d'immenses fenêtres –éléments caractéristiques des résidences de ce quartier–. Cinq pièces entières abritent environ 40.000 ouvrages. Afin d'avoir suffisamment d'espace de vie et de rangement pour ses livres, le propriétaire a dû réunir deux appartements. D'immenses bibliothèques –certaines réalisées par le propriétaire en personne– permettent d'accueillir cette quantité impressionnante d'ouvrages. Certains livres d'art trônent sur des tables, des peintures originales décorent les murs de l'appartement, à l'instar d'une galerie d'exposition. Dans la bibliothèque principale, la fresque de plafond est l'œuvre de Burt Irvin, artiste anglais. Dans cet appartement la technologie n'a pas sa place et c'est en vain que vous chercherez poste de télévision ou de radio.

Diese Wohnung liegt im Zentrum von Berlin und besticht besonders durch ihre hohen Decken, den Original Parkettboden und große Fenster –alles typische Details der Wohnungen in diesem Stadtteil. In fünf der Zimmer sind fast 40.000 Bücher untergebracht worden. Die einzige Lösung, wie man so viele Bücher verstauen und gleichzeitig noch Platz zum Wohnen schaffen konnte, war, zwei Appartements zusammenzulegen. Die Bücher wurden in riesige Regale gestellt, die der Besitzer zum Teil selbst gezimmert hat. Einige der Bücher liegen offen auf den Tischen und an den Wände hängen Originalbilder, die zu kleinen Ausstellungen einladen. Die Deckenmalerei in der Hauptbibliothek wurde vom englischen Künstler Burt Irvin gestaltet. Moderne Technologie sowie Radio und Fernsehen findet man in dieser Wohnung nicht.

The almost 40.000 books are stored in huge bookcases, some of them built by the resident himself.

Près de 40.000 livres sont rangés dans d'immenses bibliothèques dont certaines sont réalisées par le propriétaire lui-même.

Die fast 40.000 Bücher wurden in riesige Regale gestellt, einige davon sind vom Besitzer selbst gezimmert.

Original painting decorating the apartment, emphasized by the white walls and the large amount of light, coming in through the windows.

Les peintures originales, qui décorent l'appartement, sont mises en valeur par les murs blancs et l'abondance de lumière naturelle qui provient des fenêtres.

Das Appartement wurde mit Originalbildern dekoriert, die vor der weißen Wand und durch das einfallende Tageslicht besonders schön zur Geltung kommen.

Sampaoli Residence
Résidence Sampaoli
Sampaoli Residenz

Padua, Italy

This loft, set inside an old print shop that was formerly used as a carpentry warehouse, is located in a building in the city center. The main entrance passes through a garage that leads to the studio or to the residence, resolving the issue of parking while creating an unusual and informal entrance. The extensive space containing the living room, dining room, and kitchen is bathed in light due to the large windows and light-colored walls. As in the rest of the residence, traces of its former industrial use are visible: the brick walls, the exposed pipes, the pillars painted white, and the strip of glass blocks in the upper section. The sleeping area is marked off by walls and doors, as in a conventional residence, and includes two bedrooms and two bathrooms. The materials give the space a homogeneous and natural appearance. Maple wood was applied on the living room floor and smooth, while enamel-painted concrete painted was used in the kitchen and bathrooms.

Ce loft, installé à l'intérieur d'une ancienne imprimerie, autrefois un entrepôt de menuiserie, fait partie d'un édifice du centre de la cité. L'entrée principale passe sous un garage et mène au studio ou à la résidence. Cette entrée originale et informelle résout également la question du parking. L'immense espace intégrant le salon, la salle à manger et la cuisine, est inondé de lumière grâce aux grandes fenêtres et aux murs de couleurs pâles. Toute la résidence est imprégnée des traces de son passé industriel : murs de briques, tuyauterie apparente, piliers peints en blanc et bande de blocs de verre au niveau supérieur. La partie chambre est délimitée de manière conventionnelle par des murs et des portes et comprend deux chambres à coucher et deux salles de bains. Grâce aux matériaux employés, l'espace est homogène et naturel. Du bois d'érable pour le parquet du salon et du béton enduit de peinture vernie pour la cuisine et les salles de bains.

Dieser Wohnsitz, der in einer alten Druckerei eingerichtet wurde liegt in einem Gebäude im Zentrum. Der Haupteingang befindet sich in einer Garage und führt zum Studio oder dem Wohnbereich. So wird gleichzeitig das Parkplatzproblem gelöst und ein ungewöhnlich informeller Eingangsbereich geschaffen. Der extensive Raum mit Wohnzimmer, Esszimmer und Küche wird ob der großen Fenster und hellen Wände mit Licht durchflutet. Einzelne Details der vorherigen gewerblichen Nutzung sind in den Entwurf integriert worden: die Ziegelwand, die sichtbaren Rohe, die weiß gestrichenen Stützpfeiler und die Glassteine im oberen Bereich. Der Schlafbereich ist mit Wänden und Türen abgetrennt und umfasst zwei Schlaf- und zwei Badezimmer. Das Material verleiht dem Raum ein homogenes und natürliches Ambiente. Die Böden des Wohnzimmers sind mit Ahornholz ausgelegt, in der Küche und den Bädern wurde der Betonboden weiß gestrichen.

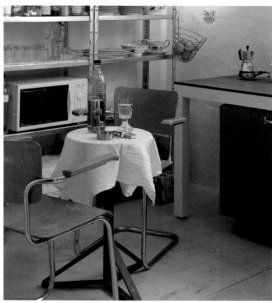

This interior's casual and informal image was achieved through the combination of austere furnishings designed by the owner of the residence.

L'image informelle de l'intérieur est née de l'association entre l'austérité de l'ameublement et les œuvres conçues par le propriétaire de la résidence.

Das informelle Ambiente im Inneren wurde durch die Kombination strenger Möbel unterstrichen, die von den Besitzern selber entworfen wurden.

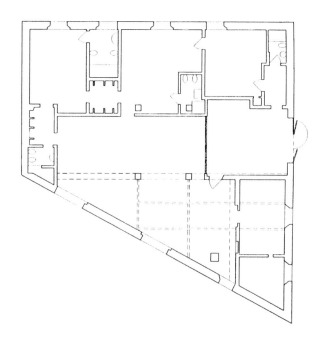

› Plan Plan Grundriss

Cloe House
Maison Cloe
Cloe Haus

Barcelona, Spain

This family house is located on a street of low houses and is spread over three levels. The first contains the entrance, living area, kitchen, and terrace. The main bedroom, lounge and studio are located on the second floor, with the children's and guest bedrooms and terrace on the top. The project's primary element is the sculptural staircase that connects the three levels and runs alongside and parallel to the main façade. This staircase organizes and divides the different areas both horizontally and vertically. On the second floor, the studio has a work table placed along the wall, perpendicular to the façade windows giving on to a small balcony. There is abundant natural light in this work space, which is characterized by simple furniture, pale colors, and its separation from the other areas of the home.

Cette demeure familiale fait partie d'une rue aux maisons basses et s'étend sur trois étages. Le premier abrite l'entrée, l'espace de vie, la cuisine et la terrasse. La chambre à coucher principale, le salon et le studio sont au deuxième étage, enfin les chambres des enfants, des amis et la terrasse sont tout en haut. L'escalier sculptural qui relie les trois niveaux entre eux et qui court en parallèle le long de la façade principale, est l'élément clé du projet. Cet escalier distribue et divise les différentes zones à la verticale comme à l'horizontale. Au second étage, le studio possède un plan de travail placé le long du mur, perpendiculaire aux fenêtres de façade donnant sur un petit balcon. Cet espace de travail est inondé de lumière. Il se définit par un mobilier simple, des couleurs pâles et le fait d'être séparé des autres zones de la maison.

Dieser Familienwohnsitz liegt im Stadtviertel in einer Straße mit niedrigen Gebäuden. Das Haus ist über drei Ebenen ausgelegt. Auf der Ersten befinden sich Eingang, Wohnbereich, Küche und eine Terrasse. Das Elternschlafzimmer, eine Lounge und ein Studio wurden in der zweiten Ebene untergebracht und Kinder- sowie Gästeschlafzimmer und eine weitere Terrasse liegen darüber. Herausragendes Element ist die Treppe, die alle drei Ebenen miteinander verbindet und parallel zur Hauptfassade gebaut wurde. Auf der zweiten Ebene ist ein Arbeitstisch direkt an der Wand installiert, mit Blick auf einen kleinen Balkon. Hier fällt viel Tageslicht ein, einfache Möbel und sanfte Farben trennen den Bereich von den anderen ab.

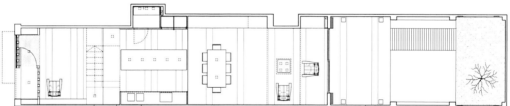

› Ground floor   Rez-de-chaussée   Erdgeschoss

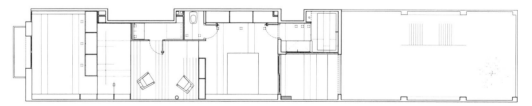

› First floor   Premier étage   Erstes Obergeschoss

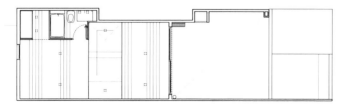

› Second floor   Deuxième étage   Zweits Obergeschoss

House in Stockholm
Maison à Stockholm
Haus in Stockholm

Stockholm, Sweden

This house was designed as both a home and a studio for a textile designer. The architects decided to divide it on two levels; they installed a dining room, kitchen, bedroom, two bathrooms and a dressing room, and left ample space for the studio and office. In spatial terms, the architects envisioned a duplex with a large, open vertical section containing a staircase and a two-story central area, which would benefit the dining room. The project's main premise was the avoidance of dividers and doors and the consequent redistribution of space by means of walls with openings that enhance visual interconnections. These partitions create a rich pattern of planes and volumes and give the project a dynamic edge. Wood is the key material throughout the home. The floor is made of oak with a white varnish, even in the kitchen. Larch is used on the terrace, while the furniture, designed by the architects themselves, is made of pine.

La maison est conçue pour abriter le domicile et le studio d'un designer textile. Les architectes ont réparti l'espace sur deux niveaux. Ils ont installé une salle à manger, une cuisine, une chambre, deux salles de bains et un dressing en laissant beaucoup d'espace pour le studio et le bureau. Sur le plan spatial, les architectes ont conçu un escalier et une aire centrale sur deux étages au profit du salon. Le critère essentiel du projet est d'éviter cloisons et portes et de redistribuer l'espace par des murs dotés d'ouvertures pour accentuer l'interconnexion visuelle. Ces cloisons créent diverses compositions de plans et volumes et imprègnent le projet de dynamisme. Le bois est le matériau clé de la maison. Le sol en chêne, recouvert d'un vernis blanc, s'étend jusque dans la cuisine. La terrasse est en mélèze et les meubles, conçus par les architectes, sont en pin.

Dieses Haus wurde als Wohnung mit integriertem Studio für einen Textildesigner konzipiert. Auf zwei Ebenen finden Esszimmer, Küche, Schlafzimmer, zwei Badezimmer sowie ein Ankleidezimmer Platz, aber auch ein Studio und das Büro. Die Architekten wünschten sich ein Doppelhaus mit einem großen, offenen, vertikalen Bereich, mit einem Treppenhaus und einem zweistöckigen Zentralbereich, in dem das Esszimmer liegt. Hauptvorgabe bei diesem Projekt war das Vermeiden von Trennwänden und Türen sowie die Neuverteilung des Raumes durch Wände mit Durchbrüchen. Diese visuellen Verbindungen schaffen ein reichhaltiges Muster an Fläche und Volumen und verleihen dem Projekt eine dynamische Note. Wichtigstes Baumaterial ist Holz. Der Boden ist durchgehend aus weiß lackierter Eiche gelegt. Die Terrasse ist aus Lärchenholz, während die von den Architekten entworfenen Möbel aus Kiefernholz gefertigt wurden.

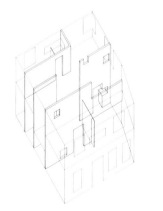

› Perspective Perspective Perspektivzeichnung

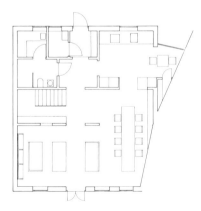

› Ground floor Rez-de-chaussée Erdgeschoss

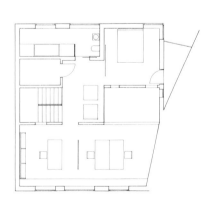

› First floor Premier étage Erstes Obergeschoss

The vertical partitions have small openings which connect the different areas in the house. The two-story space around the stairs strengthens the striking visual relationships.

Les cloisons verticales sont dotées de petites ouvertures inattendues qui créent le lien visuel entre les différentes zones de la maison. L'articulation de l'espace sur deux niveaux renforce l'intensité de la connexion visuelle.

Die vertikalen Trennwände weisen unerwartete Durchbrüche auf. Der zweigeschossige Raum um die Treppen verleiht der intensiven visuellen Verbindung Tiefe.

The true luxury of the project is its luminosity and spaciousness, rather than the decorative objects. Moreover, the harmoniousness of the building bestows serenity on the entire project.

Ce qui fait le luxe de ce projet, c'est davantage la luminosité et l'ampleur de l'espace que les objets qui le décorent. L'harmonie de la construction lui confère une sensation de calme.

Der wahre Luxus dieses Projektes ist seine Helligkeit und Weitläufigkeit. Die Harmonie des Gebäudes verleiht dem gesamten Projekt eine gewisse Klarheit und Ruhe.

House in Florence
Maison à Florence
Haus in Florenz

Florence, Italy

This house is set in a rural landscape, just outside the city. The house is accessible via two paths: the first leads to the door of an art workshop, and the other to the main residence. A wooden staircase, a green path, and an old well lead the way to the garden that encloses the north side of the building. The lower level, which houses a studio and bedroom, was designed to grant independence to each function, and highlights the main features of the construction: the height, the skylight, the trusses, and the luminosity. The skylight, the horizontal division of the volume, and the exposed wooden beams all convey the idea of a workshop. The materials used—mainly steel, cement, plaster, and glass—are strictly functional and are left untreated.

Cette résidence se situe dans un paysage rural, juste à l'extérieur de la cité. Deux chemins permettent d'accéder à la maison : le premier mène à la porte d'un atelier d'art et l'autre, à la résidence principale. Un escalier de bois et un vieux moulin conduisent au jardin qui entoure le côté nord du bâtiment. La conception du niveau inférieur, abritant un studio et une chambre, respecte l'indépendance des fonctions et exalte les caractéristiques principales de la construction : la hauteur, le velux, les poutres et la luminosité. Le velux, la division horizontale du volume et les poutres de bois apparentes, donnent l'impression d'être dans un atelier. Les matériaux employés –surtout l'acier, le ciment, le plâtre et le verre– sont purement fonctionnels et ne sont pas traités.

Dieses Haus wurde auf dem Land eingerichtet, unmittelbar ausserhalb der Stadt. Zwei Wege führen zum Haus: der erste zur Tür eines Kunstwerkraums und der andere zum Hauptgebäude. Eine Holztreppe, ein grüner Pfad und eine alte Quelle führen zum Garten an der Nordseite des Gebäudes. Das Untergeschoss mit Studio und Schlafzimmer ist so entworfen, dass beide Bereiche unabhängig voneinander genutzt werden können und die wichtigsten Merkmale des Baus unterstrichen sind: seine Höhe, die Dachfenster, die Bünde und die Helligkeit. Das Dachfenster, die horizontale Unterteilung des Gebäudes und die sichtbaren Holzbalken unterstreichen das Ambiente einer Werkstatt. Das verwendete Material, hauptsächlich Stahl, Zement, Gips und Glas, wurde rein funktionell eingesetzt und unbehandelt belassen.

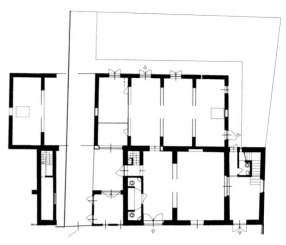

› Ground floor Rez-de-chaussée Erdgeschoss

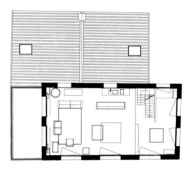

› First floor Premier étage Erstes Obergeschoss

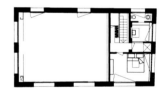

› Second floor Deuxième étage Zweits Obergeschoss

The skylight, the horizontal division of the volume, and the exposed wooden beams all help to maintain the atmosphere of a workshop.

Le velux, la division horizontale du volume et les poutres de bois apparentes contribuent à conserver l'atmosphère d'un atelier.

Das Dachfenster, die horizontale Unterteilung des Gebäudes und die sichtbaren Holzbalken unterstreichen das Ambiente eines Ateliers.

206

The materials used, mainly steel, cement, plaster, and black wood, are untreated and simple, both in terms of appearance and function.

Les matériaux employés, surtout l'acier, le ciment, le plâtre et le bois noir sont bruts et simples tant sur le plan de l'aspect que de la fonction.

Das verwendete Material, Edelstahl, Zement, Gips und schwarzes Holz, wirkt natürlich und einfach sowohl im Hinblick auf Aussehen als auch auf Funktion.

Loft in Milan
Loft à Milan
Loft in Mailand

Milan, Italy

The reformation of this loft entailed combining two autonomous units into a single unified and flexible space. The result is a large residence, defined by its two main elements: an area embracing the living room, dining room, and library; and the realm of the private spaces, such as the bathrooms, the dressing room, and the bedroom. A columnar system organizes the home, although their structural regularity has been broken by the insertion of small cubes. The entrance was planned as a small area off the passageway between the kitchen and bathroom that leads to the dining room. The office is concealed behind a wooden closet at the end of the hall, between the entrance and the living room. One of the walls is mounted with shelves, thus transforming the corridor into a library. The architects designed some of the loft's furnishings and thereby added touches of color to set off the white walls.

La rénovation de ce loft consiste à combiner deux unités autonomes dans un seul espace unifié et modulable. Il en résulte une grande résidence définie par deux éléments principaux : un espace abritant le salon, la salle à manger et la bibliothèque et le royaume des espaces privés, à l'instar des salles de bains, du dressing et de la chambre à coucher. L'espace s'articule autour d'un système de colonnes dont on a rompu la régularité structurelle en insérant des petits cubes. L'entrée est un petit espace entre la cuisine et la salle de bains qui mène à la salle à manger. Le bureau est escamoté derrière une armoire au bout du hall, entre l'entrée et le salon. Un des murs est garni d'étagères, transformant le couloir en bibliothèque. Les architectes ont conçu certains éléments du mobilier du loft, ajoutant ainsi des touches de couleur qui rehaussent les murs blancs.

Bei der Renovierung dieses Lofts wurden zwei unabhängige Einheiten zu einem einzigen, flexiblen Raum verbunden. Das Ergebnis ist ein großer Wohnraum, den zwei Hauptelemente definieren: ein Bereich, der das Wohnzimmer, Esszimmer und eine Bibliothek umfasst sowie einen weiteren mit Bad, Ankleide- und Schlafzimmer. Ein System von Säulen strukturiert das Haus, wobei das Einfügen kleiner Würfel die Gleichmäßigkeit durchbricht. Der Eingang, der zum Esszimmer führt, wurde als kleiner Bereich außerhalb des Flurs zwischen Küche und Bad geplant. Das Büro liegt verdeckt hinter einem Holzschrank am Ende des Flurs zwischen Eingang und Wohnzimmer. Eine Wand ist mit Regalen ausgestattet, der Flur dient so als Bibliothek. Die Architekten haben einen Teil der Möbel selbst entworfen und damit Farbtupfer innerhalb der weißen Wände geschaffen.

The architects designed some of the loft's furnishings with the aim of adding a touch of color to set off the white walls.

Les architectes ont dessiné certaines pièces du mobilier du loft dans le but d'ajouter une touche de couleur pour mettre en valeur les murs blancs.

Die Architekten haben einen Teil der Möbel selbst entworfen und so Farbtupfer innerhalb der weißen Wände geschaffen.

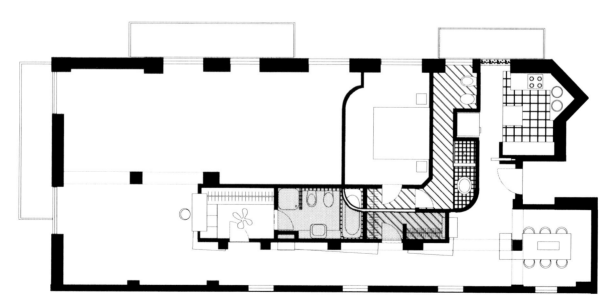

› Plan Plan Grundriss

Renovated Apartment
Appartement rénové
Renoviertes Appartement

Berlin, Germany

A series of architectural interventions transformed a typical Berlin art nouveau apartment spatially and programmatically. The first step was a large horizontal cut between the central room and new kitchen, allowing these two spaces to be unified. Traditionally, a service kitchen was designated to the rear of the apartment. The public living and workspaces are oriented to the street including a small children's room. The side wing is organized as a private area of bedrooms and baths. A steel framed screen wall of translucent glass and birch plywood bringing light to the dark corridor and replacing the non-bearing historical corridor wall. Doors were replaced with large sliding panels and all remaining significant historical finishes, details, and hardware were left intact. New construction is made distinct through a material palette of sealed warm-rolled steel, stainless steel and birch plywood.

Diverses modifications architecturales apportées à cet appartement style Art Nouveau, typiquement berlinois, en ont changé la distribution spatiale. La première étape a été d'éliminer la séparation entre la pièce centrale et la cuisine pour les réunir en un seul espace. Désormais, le salon et les espaces bureau sont orientés vers la rue y compris une petite chambre d'enfant. L'aile latérale abrite la partie privée qui s'articule autour des chambres à coucher et des salles de bains. Une partition murale en verre translucide, encadrée d'acier et en contreplaqué de bouleau, illumine le couloir sombre et se substitue au mur traditionnel sans fonction portante. Les portes ont été remplacées par de grandes cloisons coulissantes et toutes les finitions, détails et ferrures anciennes ont été conservées. La rénovation se décline visuellement dans une palette de matériaux conjuguant acier laminé thermique étanche, acier inoxydable et contreplaqué de bouleau.

Ein typisches Appartement im Stil des Art Nouveau in Berlin wurde durch eine Reihe von architektonischen Interventionen von Grund auf umgestaltet. Zunächst wurden das zentrale Wohnzimmer und die neue Küche horizontal durch einen langen Schnitt geöffnet und diese beiden Räume so miteinander vereint. Die Küche lag vorher im hinteren Ende des Appartements. Die öffentlichen Wohn- und Arbeitsplätze weisen neben einem kleinen Kinderzimmer auf die Straße. Der Seitenflügel ist als privater Bereich den Schlaf- und Badezimmern vorbehalten. Eine mit Stahl gerahmte Trennwand aus Glas und Birkenholz lässt Licht in den dunklen Flur einfallen. Die Türen wurden durch große Schiebewände ersetzt und alle wichtigen historischen Details blieben weitgehend erhalten. Die neue Konstruktion zeichnet sich vor allem durch das Material aus: wärmegehärteter Stahl, Edelstahl und Birkensperrholz.

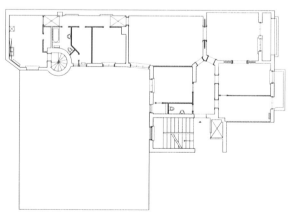

› Plan Plan Grundriss

To emphasize the feeling of continuity, all the doors were replaced by large sliding panels.

Pour exalter la sensation de continuité, toutes les portes ont été remplacées par de grands panneaux coulissants.

Um das Gefühl von Kontinuität zu verstärken, wurden alle Türen durch große Schiebewände ersetzt.

Christophe Pillet Apartment

Appartement de Christophe Pillet

Appartement von Christophe Pillet

Paris, France

Christophe Pillet designed his Paris residence, an apartment with a studio, in which he could both live and work. The renovation was based on three principles: taking out as many walls as possible to provide the maximum space; cleaning and preserving the structure; and painting the entire house white. The home revolves around two basic spaces: the living room/dining room and, on another level, the two-room studio. The latter has been decorated with the same simplicity that Pillet brought to the rest of the house. His workspace is an L-shaped table, set against the wall with an easel in front. Throughout the house, Pillet preserved the original woodwork of the window frames—now painted white—, the radiators with exposed pipes, and the wooden daises. The furniture in the living/dining room consists of selected pieces by well known designers, such as the RAR chairs by Charles and Ray Eames, a Jaobsen table and a Sotssas lamp.

Christophe Pillet, a conçu lui-même sa résidence parisienne, un appartement avec un studio pour y vivre et y travailler. La restauration suit trois lignes directrices : ôter le plus possible de murs pour un maximum d'espace, nettoyer et préserver la structure existante et peindre toute la maison en blanc. Le logement s'articule autour de deux espaces essentiels : le salon/salle à manger et sur un autre niveau, le studio deux pièces. Ce dernier est imprimé du sceau de la simplicité dont Pillet a marqué le reste de la maison. Son plan de travail est une table en L placée contre le mur, face à un chevalet. Dans toute la maison, Pillet a gardé les boiseries d'origine encadrant les fenêtres –peintes en blanc–, les radiateurs avec la tuyauterie apparente et les estrades de bois. Les meubles du salon/salle à manger sont des pièces uniques de designers de renom, comme les chaises RAR par Charles et Ray Eames, une table Jacobsen et une lampe Sotssas.

Christophe Pillet hat seine Pariser Residenz selbst entworfen: ein großes Appartement mit Studio. Die Renovierung basierte auf folgenden drei Grundsätzen: So viele Wände wie möglich herausnehmen, um den Raum zu vergrößern; die Struktur reinigen und erhalten; das gesamte Haus weiß anstreichen. Die Wohnung ist in 2 Bereiche unterteilt: das Wohn-/Esszimmer sowie auf einer weiteren Ebene das Studio mit zwei Zimmern. Der Arbeitsplatz ist ein Tisch in L-Form, der, wie auch die Staffelei, vor einer Wand steht. Im gesamten Haus hat Pillet die Holzarbeiten der Fensterrahmen im Original beibehalten (weiß gestrichen), ebenso wie die Heizungen mit den Rohren und die hölzernen Blumen. Das Mobiliar im Wohn-/Esszimmer besteht aus ausgewählten Teilen bekannter Designer, wie z.B. RAR-Stühle von Charles und Ray Eames, ein Tisch von Jacobsen und eine Lampe von Sotssas.

In this home belonging to a highly reputed French designer, a neutral, flexible atmosphere predominates, ideal for accommodating many contrasting design elements: most are created by the owner himself.

La maison de ce grand designer français est dominée par une atmosphère neutre et flexible, idéale pour y installer un grand nombre d'éléments de design contrastés : la plupart des modèles sont l'œuvre même du propriétaire.

In der Residenz des bekannten französischen Designers dominiert ein neutrales, flexibles Ambiente. Hier ist Platz für viele Designelemente, vom Besitzer entworfene Prototypen.

A glass window inserted in the ceiling allows natural light to enter and creates a warm effect, enhanced by the wooden flooring.

Un vitrage inséré dans le plafond permet à la lumière naturelle de pénétrer et d'inonder l'espace ainsi que les sols recouverts de parquet pour créer une ambiance chaleureuse.

Ein Dachfenster erlaubt den Einfall von Tageslicht und sorgt gemeinsam mit dem Holzboden für ein urgemütliches Ambiente.

Lakeside Studio
Atelier à côté du lac
Studio am See

Kloten, Switzerland

The aim was to capture the best views of Lake Maggiore, so this building was designed in the form of a tower that was predominately vertical. The structural walls are made of concrete, while the interior walls are made with insulated panels that are lighter and more flexible. The cladding on the exterior, made up of narrow wooden boards, emphasizes the verticality of the building even more, while a west-facing balcony acts as a horizontal counterpoint. The high ceilings and large windows emphasize the feeling of spaciousness and allow sunlight to pour in from the lake area. The position on the highest part of a hill represented a construction challenge, because there was no existing entrance from the highway.

Comme il fallait saisir les meilleures vues sur le Lac Majeur, cet édifice a été conçu sous la forme d'une tour caractérisée par sa verticalité. Si les murs de soutien sont en béton, les murs intérieurs sont revêtus de panneaux isolants, plus légers et flexibles. Le revêtement extérieur, composé de lattes de bois étroites, accentue davantage encore la verticalité de la construction, interrompue par un balcon, à l'ouest, agissant comme contrepoint. Les hauts plafonds et les grandes fenêtres exaltent la sensation d'espace et laissent la lumière de la région du lac inonder les pièces. Situé sur la cime de la colline, la construction est un véritable défi architectural, vu qu'il n'y a pas d'entrée depuis la route principale.

Ziel war es, den schönsten Blick auf den Lago Maggiore zu erhaschen, das Gebäude wurde also in Form eines Turms konzipiert. Die tragenden Wände sind aus Beton gefertigt, die Innenwände aus Isolierplatten, die leichter und flexibler sind. Das Haus wurde außen mit schmalen Holzbrettern verkleidet. Diese verstärken den vertikalen Eindruck des Gebäudes, während ein nach westen weisender Balkon als horizontales Gegengewicht wirkt. Die hohen Decken und großen Fenster unterstützen das Gefühl von Weite und ermöglichen den Einfall von Sonnenlicht. Die Lage auf dem höchsten Punkt eines Hügels stellte eine echte Herausforderung an den Bau dar, da es keinen direkten Zugang von der Straße gibt.

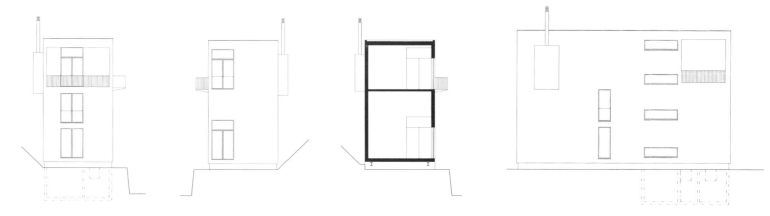

› Elevations Élévations Aufrisse

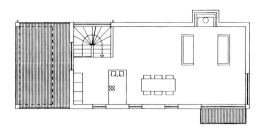

› **Ground floor** Rez-de-chaussée Erdgeschoss

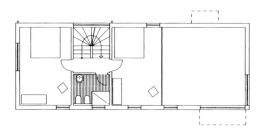

› **First floor** Premier étage Erstes Obergeschoss

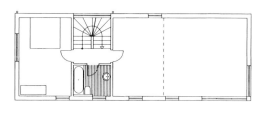

› **Second floor** Deuxième étage Zweits Obergeschoss

House-workshop
Maison atelier
Haus und Atelier

Berlin, Germany

The owner purchased this apartment at the end of the planning stage and so had the opportunity to participate decisively in its conception. Bearing in mind her individual needs, this designer of glass objects decided to fit a small studio into the apartment and put her workshop in the basement. The studio is separated from the rest of the domestic space by a huge closet on castors. The workshop is reached via an elevator that opens directly onto the apartment. The living room and bathroom are visually connected with each other by a small window. Huge, floor-to-ceiling windows surround the whole apartment and offer magnificent views over the city. The whole apartment is decorated by the artworks of the owner, and together with some furniture pieces like the violet bed, they contrast with the white walls and the white flooring, creating blazing effects.

Le propriétaire de cet appartement en a fait l'acquisition en fin de planification ce qui lui a permis de participer aux décisions conceptuelles finales. Connaissant ses besoins personnels, ce designer d'objets de verre a décidé d'intégrer un petit studio à cet appartement et d'installer son atelier au sous-sol. Le studio est séparé de l'espace privé par une immense armoire sur roulettes. L'ascenseur, qui s'ouvre directement sur l'appartement, mène à l'atelier. Une petite fenêtre établit le lien visuel entre le salon et la salle de bains. D'immenses fenêtres tout en hauteur font le tour de l'appartement et offrent de superbes vues sur la cité. Les œuvres d'art du propriétaire ornent l'appartement et, conjuguées à certains meubles à l'instar du lit violet, tranchent avec les murs et les sols blancs, créant des effets extraordinaires.

Die Eigentümerin hat dieses Appartement am Ende der Planungsphase erworben und konnte so entscheidend in seine Konzeption mit eingreifen. Um ihren eigenen Anforderungen gerecht zu werden, entschied die Designerin von Glasobjekten, ein kleines Studio in das Appartement einzubauen und ihr Atelier im Keller unterzubringen. Das Studio ist durch einen riesigen Schrank auf Rollen vom Wohnraum getrennt. Das Atelier erreicht man über einen Aufzug, der direkt in das Appartement führt. Wohnzimmer und Bad sind durch ein kleines Fenster visuell miteinander verbunden. Große, vom Boden bis zur Decke reichende Fenster bieten herrliche Ausblicke auf die Stadt Berlin. Das gesamte Appartement ist mit Kunstwerken der Bewohnerin geschmückt. Einzelne Möbelstücke, wie das violette Bett, kontrastieren mit den weißen Wänden und Bodenfliesen und bilden interessante Effekte.

The colored furniture pieces contrast with the white walls and floors and create blazing effects.

Les meubles de couleur contrastent avec la blancheur des murs et des sols et créent des effets éblouissants.

Die farbigen Möbelstücke kontrastieren mit den weißen Wänden und Böden, was zu verblüffenden Effekten führt.

Huge, floor-to-ceiling windows surround the whole apartment and offer magnificent views over the city of Berlin.

D'immenses fenêtres, tout en hauteur, font le tour de l'appartement et offrent de superbes vues sur Berlin.

Große, vom Boden bis zur Decke reichende Fenster bieten herrliche Ausblicke auf die Stadt Berlin.

House in Barcelona
Maison à Barcelone
Haus in Barcelona

Barcelona, Spain

This project transformed a typical apartment into a single-space studio and residence. Many such apartments have been converted into loft-style living spaces that take advantage of the building's placement to obtain the best light. Partitions, corridors, and bedrooms were eliminated to create a spacious area divided by large sliding doors and integrate a graphic design studio into the living space. The incorporation of a work-space into the home determined the installation of folding and sliding translucent glass doors on wooden frames that distinguish between private and professional areas. The studio was laid out in such a way that it can be easily opened on to the living area and become a continuation of the private space. The furniture in the work area consists of open bookcases, sturdy tables, and a book-shelf around the perimeter of the studio and living area that is an attractive space-saving device. The studio also has access to an exterior terrace.

Ce projet permet de transformer un apparte-ment typique en un studio d'une pièce et une rési-dence. De nombreux appartements de ce genre ont été transformés en lofts qui grâce à l'emplace-ment de l'édifice bénéficient d'une meilleure lumière. Cloisons, couloirs et chambres disparais-sent au profit d'un large espace de vie divisé par de grandes portes coulissantes et intégrant un studio de design graphique. L'intégration d'une aire de travail au cœur de la maison a pu se faire par l'installation de portes de verre translucide coulissantes et pliantes, montées sur châssis de bois, pour séparer les sphères professionnelles et privées. Le studio est conçu de façon à s'ouvrir aisément sur le salon, en prolongement de la sphère privée. Le mobilier de l'espace de travail décline bibliothèque ouverte, tables robustes et une étagère qui fait le tour du studio et du salon, gain de place élégant et pratique. Le studio peut aussi accéder à la terrasse extérieure.

Bei dem Projekt wurde ein typisches Apparte-ment in Barcelona in ein Studio mit Wohnbereich verwandelt. Viele solcher Appartements sind in Lofts umgebaut unter Einbezug der Ausrichtung des Gebäudes, um so viel Tageslicht wie möglich zu erhalten. Trennwände, Flure und Schlafzimmer wurden aufgelöst, um einen weiträumigen Bereich zu schaffen, der durch Schiebetüren getrennt wird und im Wohnbereich eingebunden ist. Durchsichtige Falt- und Glasschiebetüren auf hölzernen Rahmen trennen privat und beruflich genutzte Bereiche. Das Studio kann zum Wohn-bereich hin geöffnet werden und so den Privatbe-reich vergrößern. Die Möbel im Arbeitsbereich bestehen aus offenen Regalen, robusten Tischen und einem Bücherregal rund um das Studio und den Wohnbereich. Das Studio führt außerdem auf eine Terrasse.

The furniture and display chosen for the work area consists of open bookcases and sturdy tables. It also leads on to an exterior terrace.

Le mobilier et l'agencement de la pièce de travail sont constitués d'une bibliothèque ouverte et de tables robustes. Le bureau s'ouvre sur une terrasse extérieure.

Die Möbel für den Arbeitsbereich bestehen aus offenen Regalen und stabilen Arbeitstischen. Der Arbeitsbereich weist zudem auf eine Terrasse hinaus.

The folding and sliding wood-framed, translucent glass doors mark the boundary between the private and professional areas.

Les portes de verre coulissantes à battants et encadrées de bois définissent la partie privée et la partie professionnelle.

Die Glasfalt- und Schiebetüren mit hölzernem Rahmen trennen die privat und beruflich genutzten Bereiche voneinander ab.

House Maske-Faini
Maison Maske-Faini
Haus Maske-Faini

Berlin, Germany

The color scheme and the confluence of art and architecture both play important roles in this mansion house, the home of the architect Anna Maske and the artist Fausto Faini. Maske has created a miniature architecture for her daughter: a tiny world with two shops and the facades of streets and courtyards, made from her own designs and hand-painted by Gio Ponti: it is a space that encourages experimentation and improvisation. The other four inner rooms and the workshop are interconnected but they also have their own independent exit onto the corridor. The workshop itself is a all white painted room with a large window on one side, allowing the natural light to flow in and thus offering perfect conditions for a painting studio. The doors in the entrance are from the Art Nouveau era and combined with the more modern wall decorations and floor coverings, they create an animating contrast and bring a touch of sophistication into the dwelling.

Dans cette demeure, la maison de l'architecte Anna Maske et de l'artiste Fausto Faini, la gamme des couleurs et la rencontre entre l'art et l'architecture jouent un rôle prépondérant. Maske a créé une architecture miniature pour sa fille : un petit univers avec deux magasins et les façades sur les rues et des cours intérieures, fruit de son design personnel et peint à la main par Gio Ponti. C'est un espace pour expérimenter et improviser. Les quatre autres pièces intérieures sont reliées à l'atelier tout en ayant leur propre entrée et couloir. L'atelier est une pièce entièrement peinte en blanc dotée d'une grande fenêtre latérale qui laisse pénétrer la lumière du jour, conditions idéales pour un atelier de peintre. Les portes d'entrée Art Nouveau, associées aux décorations murales et aux revêtements des sols plus modernes, créent un contraste intéressant et apportent une touche d'élégance à la demeure.

Das Farbschema und das Zusammenspiel von Kunst und Architektur spielen eine wichtige Rolle in diesem Herrenhaus, dem Wohnsitz der Architektin Anna Maske und dem Künstler Fausto Faini. Maske hat dabei eine Miniarchitektur für ihre Tochter geschaffen: Eine kleine Welt mit zwei Läden und Fassaden von Straßen und Innenhöfen, die nach eigenen Entwürfen angefertigt und von Gio Ponti von Hand bemalt wurden. Die anderen vier Innenräume und das Atelier sind miteinander verbunden, verfügen jedoch auch über einen eigenen Ausgang auf den Flur. Das Atelier selbst ist ein weiß gestrichener Raum mit einem großen Fenster, das natürliches Tageslicht hereinlässt und so die idealen Bedingungen für ein Malstudio bietet. Die Türen im Eingang stammen noch aus dem Art Nouveau und bilden gemeinsam mit den eher modernen Wanddekorationen und Bodenbelägen einen belebenden Kontrast und einen Hauch von Raffinesse.

All rooms are interconnected but also have their own independent exit onto the corridor.

Toutes les pièces sont reliées entre elles avec, toutefois, un couloir et une entrée indépendantes.

Alle Zimmer sind miteinander verbunden, verfügen aber auch über einen eigenen Ausgang auf den Flur.

The color scheme plays an important role in this mansion house, the home of the architect Anna Maske and the artist Fausto Faini.

La gamme de couleurs joue un rôle prépondérant dans cette demeure, logis de l'architecte Anna Maske et de l'artiste Fausto Faini.

Das Farbschema spielt eine wichtige Rolle in diesem Herrenhaus, dem Wohnsitz der Architektin Anna Maske und dem Künstler Fausto Faini.

Getter House
Maison Getter
Getter Haus

Tel-Aviv, Israel

Intense colors and a focus on fun stand out in this penthouse decorated by its owner. The intensity of color is especially strong in the kitchen and dining area, which has an extensive wall decorated in strong tones like yellow, apple green, red and pink. Shapes and colors identical to those of the wall are painted on the ceiling of this room and the floor is paved in tiles of varying origins, prints, colors and sizes. On the contrary, the work area and living room have been decorated in tones that aid in the search for calm and concentration, like black, white, and the light color of the wood, the only tone used in the walls, ceilings and floors, as well as the shelves and work table. An interesting visual effect has been achieved due to the irregular placement of one of the windows—near the work table—and a large bright red chaise longue right in the center of the room.

Ce duplex, décoré par son propriétaire, est placé sous le signe des couleurs et respire la gaieté. Les couleurs sont particulièrement intenses dans la cuisine et dans la salle à manger dotée d'un grand mur qui décline une gamme de tons vifs à l'instar du jaune, du vert pomme, du rouge et du rose. Les couleurs et les formes sur le mur se répètent sur le plafond de la pièce. Le carrelage du sol est d'origines, d'impressions, de tailles et de couleurs diverses. En opposition, les tons de l'aire de travail et du salon, dans une gamme de noir et de blanc, sont plus calmes et propices à la concentration, à l'instar de la couleur claire du bois qui habille les murs, le plafond et les sols sans oublier les étagères et la table de travail. Des effets optiques intéressants sont suggérés par l'emplacement irrégulier d'une des fenêtres –près du bureau– et par une large chaise longue rouge placée juste au cœur de la pièce.

Intensive Farben und lustige Elemente fallen bei diesem Penthouse, das von seinem Besitzer persönlich ausgestattet wurde, besonders ins Auge. Die Intensität der Farben ist besonders in der Küche und dem Esszimmer präsent, wo die Wände in Farben wie Gelb, Apfelgrün, Rot und Pink bemalt sind. Einzelne Formen sowie die Farben der Wand wiederholen sich auch in der Bemalung der Decke, der Boden wurde mit Fliesen in verschiedenen Mustern, Farben und Größen ausgelegt. Der Arbeitsbereich und das Wohnzimmer sind dagegen eher in Tönen gehalten, die Ruhe und Konzentration einfordern: Schwarz, Weiß und der helle Ton der Holzbretter, mit denen Wände, Decken und Böden dekoriert, aber auch Regale und Schreibtisch geformt wurden. Einen interessanten visuellen Effekt erzielen die unregelmäßige Platzierung eines der Fenster in der Nähe des Schreibtisches und ein großer, leuchtend roter Chaiselongue mitten im Raum.

The windows, divided in rectangles create a luminous effect in the exterior as well as the interior of the house.

Les fenêtres, divisées en rectangles, créent des effets lumineux à l'intérieur comme à l'extérieur de la maison.

Die in Rechtecke unterteilten Fenster bilden sowohl im Inneren als auch in den Außenbereichen des Hauses einen lichtdurchfluteten Effekt.

250

The owner himself has restored some of the kitchen furniture—small tables, shelves and chairs.

Certains meubles de la cuisine ont été restaurés par le propriétaire lui-même –petites tables, étagères et chaises.

Der Eigentümer hat einen Teil der Küchenmöbel selbst restauriert, kleine Tische, Regale und Stühle.

Atelier in Buenos Aires
Atelier à Buenos Aires
Atelier in Buenos Aires

Buenos Aires, Argentina

This loft was previously a bakery store set in an old market. It belongs to Luis Benedit, a well-known artist and architect who decided to buy the 1,830 sq.-ft space and transform it into his own living and working space. In order to create a homely atmosphere, he clad the walls with panels of Guatambú wood and ran a quartz lighting system along the industrial ceiling grill. All the public areas were distributed over the 130-ft length of the loft. The kitchen and living area share a raised platform, to differentiate them from the remaining studio space. The use of different levels is a valuable technique for small or narrow spaces needing to create various settings. A few designer pieces, such as the office chair and red couch, add a contemporary touch, while the bathroom was fashioned out of recycled objects, such as the fancy tiles, the large washbasin, and the shelves made out of pieces of tree trunk.

Ce loft était à l'origine une ancienne boulangerie située dans un vieux marché. Son propriétaire, Luis Benedit, artiste et architecte réputé, a acheté les 170 m², pour y installer son domicile et son cabinet d'architecture. Pour une atmosphère accueillante, il a habillé les murs de lambris de bois de guatambu et installé un système d'éclairage à quartz le long de la grille de plafond d'usine. Toutes les zones publiques sont distribuées sur les 40 m du loft. La cuisine et le salon partagent une plate-forme surélevée pour les différencier du reste du studio. L'emploi de différents niveaux est une technique valable pour moduler l'agencement des espaces petits ou étriqués. Des créations de designers, comme la chaise de bureau et le divan rouge, ajoutent une touche contemporaine, contrastant avec la salle de bains constituée d'objets recyclés, à l'instar du carrelage fantaisie, du grand évier et des étagères faites de morceaux de tronc d'arbres.

Dieses Loft war vorher eine Bäckerei in einem alten Markt. Es gehört Luis Benedit, einem bekannten Künstler und Architekten, der in diesem 170 m² großen Raum sein Zuhause und seinen Arbeitsplatz einrichten wollte. Um eine gemütliche Atmosphäre zu schaffen, hat er die Wände mit Guatambu-Holz verkleidet und ein Beleuchtungssystem aus Quarz auf der industriellen Gitterdecke installiert. Alle öffentlichen Bereiche wurden entlang der gesamten 40 m Länge des Lofts verteilt. Die Küche und der Wohnbereich befinden sich auf einer Empore, um sie vom verbleibenden Studio abzusetzen. Der Einsatz von verschiedenen Ebenen ist eine beliebte Technik für kleine oder enge Räume. Ein paar Designerstücke, wie z.B. der Bürostuhl und eine rote Couch, sorgen für einen modernen Touch, während das Badezimmer mit wiederverwerteten Objekten ausgestattet wurde, wie z.B. die schönen Fliesen, das große Waschbassin und die Regale, die aus Holzstämmen gefertigt wurden.

The work area is set alongside large windows that allow natural light to flow in.

Le bureau se situe le long d'un espace doté de grandes fenêtres qui l'inondent de lumière naturelle.

Der Arbeitsbereich befindet sich an einem Ort mit großen Fenstern, dadurch fällt natürliches Tageslicht ein.

The kitchen can be seen behind a pre-existing stone wall, and the countertop was made from tiles that were found on a demolition site.

La cuisine est visible au bout d'un mur de pierre préexistent. Le haut du comptoir est recouvert de tuiles trouvées sur un site de démolition.

Die Küche liegt hinter einer schon vorhandenen Steinwand. Die Arbeitsfläche besteht aus Fliesen, die auf dem Abrissgelände herumlagen.

Wooden floors and a quartz lighting system create a homely atmosphere.

Des sols en bois et un système d'éclairage à quartz créent une atmosphère feutrée et conviviale.

Holzböden und ein Onatz- Beleuchtungssystem sorgen für angemessene Gemütlichkeit.

The bedroom features a chair designed by Benedit, an art-deco night table, and a painting by Pat Andrea.

La chambre à coucher comprend une chaise dessinée par Benedit, une table de chevet Art Déco et une peinture de Pat Andrea.

Das Schlafzimmer besticht durch einen Stuhl von Benedit, einen Art-Deco Nachttisch und ein Bild von Pat Andrea.

Cheval 2.3 House
Maison Cheval 2.3
Cheval 2.3 Haus

Berlin, Germany

This building, built at the end of the nineteenth century, was originally the headquarters of the Prussian barracks. It was later used as the temporary residence of the last Chancellor of the Reich, Paul Hindenburg, and in the mid-eighties it housed part of the International Building Exhibition. A program of repairs and restructuring resulted in the division of the 5,400-square foot home into three independent units. In one of these units, installed the creative team Cheval 2.3 and converted one of them into their home and office. The old parquet floor and the wood-paneled doors preserve characteristic features of the Wilhelminian style. Dark and heavy furniture was applied in the office area, while the living room and kitchen are equipped with light materials, bright colors and black and white checkered tiles. The white painted walls and the large windows enhance the feeling of spaciousness and make the space a warm, extraordinary home.

Ce bâtiment, construit à la fin du XIXe siècle, accueillait autrefois l'administration centrale des casernes prussiennes. Il fût utilisé plus tard en tant que résidence temporaire de Paul Hindenburg, dernier chancelier du Reich et dans la moitié des années quatre-vingt-dix, il abrita le International Building Exhibition. Des transformations et réparations ont restructuré les 500 m² en trois unités indépendantes. L'une d'entre elles a été occupée par l'équipe de créateurs Cheval 2.3 qui l'a transformée en leur habitation et leur bureau. L'ancien parquet et les lambris des portes sont des réminiscences du style de l'époque Wilhelmine. Des meubles sombres et massifs décorent l'espace bureau, alors que matériaux légers, couleurs vives et carrelage à damier noir définissent le salon et la cuisine. Les murs blancs et les grandes fenêtres exaltent la sensation d'espace et font de cette habitation un univers chaleureux extraordinaire.

Dieses Gebäude, das gegen Ende des 19. Jahrhunderts errichtet wurde, war einst preußische Kaserne und Sitz des Hauptquartiers. Es diente später zeitweilig als Aufenthaltsort des letzten Reichskanzlers Paul Hindenburg, und Mitte der 80er Jahre wurde hier ein Teil der International Building Exhibition gezeigt. Bei den Renovierungsarbeiten wurde das 500 m² große Haus in drei voneinander unabhängige Einheiten unterteilt. In einer dieser Einheiten hat sich das Kreativteam Cheval 2.3 niedargelassen, und das Loft in eine Wohnung mit Büro umgebaut. Der alte Parkettboden und die mit Holz vertäfelten Türen erinnern an den einstigen wilhelminischen Stil. Das Büro wurde mit dunklen und schweren Möbeln ausgestattet, Wohnzimmer und Küche eher mit leichtem Material, leuchtenden Farben und schwarz-weißen Fliesen. Die weiß gestrichenen Wände und großen Fenster tragen zur Geräumigkeit und zum warmen, außergewöhnlichen Ambiente bei.

The old parquet floor and the wood-paneled doors preserve characteristic features of the Wilhelminian style.

L'ancien parquet et les lambris des portes sont des réminiscences du style de l'époque Wilhelmine.

Der alte Parkettboden und die mit Holz vertäfelten Türen erinnern an den einstigen wilhelminischen Stil.

The white painted walls and the large windows enhance the feeling of spaciousness and make the space a warm, extraordinary dwelling.

Les murs blancs et les grandes fenêtres exaltent la sensation d'espace et confèrent à la demeure une ambiance empreinte de chaleur et de fantastique.

Die weiß gestrichenen Wände und großen Fenster tragen zur Geräumigkeit und zum warmen, außergewöhnlichen Ambiente bei.

Bucks County, United States

Durham Press

This rural building, formerly a schoolhouse, was converted into the home and workspace of fine art publishers Ann Marshall and Jean-Paul Russell. A master printmaker, Russell made prints for Andy Warhol in New York in the 1980s. The studio, contained within a large surface area, was separated from the living areas to prevent the spreading of fumes, odors, or paint. The innumerable jars and pots on shelves and underneath tables are always visible, for both practical and esthetic reasons. The ordered clutter of the elements endows the space with movement and character, in contrast with the more minimalist and serene appearance of the private area. Stunning works by various artists are displayed throughout the home, adding color and enhancing the mood of the different areas. High ceilings and a row of large windows heighten the sense of spaciousness and provide sufficient light for the artists' work requirements.

Cet édifice rural, une ancienne école, a été converti en lieu d'habitation et de travail pour Ann Marshall et Jean-Paul Russell, éditeurs d'art. Russell, lithographe de renom, a réalisé des gravures pour Andy Warhol, à New York, dans les années 80. Le studio, partie intégrante d'une grande surface, est séparé des zones de vie pour éviter les émanations de fumée, d'odeurs ou de peintures. Les innombrables pots et cruches sur les étagères et sous les tables sont visibles, pour des raisons esthétiques et pratiques. Le capharnaüm ordonné de tous ces éléments confère caractère et mouvement à l'espace, contrastant avec l'agencement plus minimaliste et calme de la sphère privée. De superbes œuvres de divers artistes, essaimées dans toute l'habitation, ponctuent de couleur les différentes pièces ainsi mises en valeur. Hauts plafonds et grandes fenêtres en enfilade accentuent l'impression d'espace et apportent la lumière nécessaire au travail de l'artiste.

Dieses ländliche Gebäude in Pennsylvania, ein ehemaliges Schulhaus, wurde in den Wohn- und Arbeitsbereich der Verlegerin Ann Marshall und Jean-Paul Russel, verwandelt. Russel hat u.a. in den 80er Jahren die Drucke für Andy Warhol in New York erstellt. Das Studio ist vom Wohnbereich getrennt, um das Austreten von Dämpfen, Geruch oder Farben zu verhindern. Die unzähligen Töpfe und Farbeimer auf den Regalen und unter den Tischen sind sowohl aus praktischen wie auch aus ästhetischen Erwägungen immer sichtbar. Das geordnete Chaos der einzelnen Elemente verleiht dem Raum Bewegung und Charakter, im Gegensatz zum eher minimalistischen und ernsten Ambiente der Privatbereiche. Beeindruckende Kunstwerke verschiedener Künstler finden sich in der ganzen Wohnung. Hohe Decken und eine Reihe großer Fenster sorgen für ein Gefühl von Weite und bieten ausreichend Licht für die Arbeit des Künstlers.

The studio was separated from the living areas to prevent the spreading of fumes, odors, or paint.

Le studio, installé dans une vaste surface est séparé du salon pour empêcher les émanations d'odeurs et de peinture.

Das Studio wurde vom Wohnbereich getrennt, um das Austreten von Dämpfen, Geruch oder Farben zu verhindern.

The occupants' minimalist sensibility combines with their bold and colorful work to create a balanced, dynamic space.

La sensibilité minimaliste des propriétaires alliée à leur œuvre simple et colorée engendre un espace harmonieux et dynamique.

Der Sinn für Minimalismus der Eigentümer, gepaart mit ihrer klaren und farbenfrohen Arbeit, hat einen ausgewogenen, dynamischen Raum erschaffen.

Striking works by various artists are displayed throughout the home.

Des œuvres étonnantes de différents artistes sont exposées au fil des pièces de la maison.

Beeindruckende Arbeiten verschiedener Künstler schmücken die einzelnen Zimmer.

Studio in Philadelphia
Studio à Philadelphie
Studio in Philadelphia

Philadelphia, United States

This converted textile factory in an old industrial area in the city presents an eclectic mix of styles reflecting the personality and tastes of its owner, an artist and director of a non-profit-making art gallery. The painting studio is partitioned off from the living space by an 8-ft wall, on which the owner added old, wood-framed windows in order to fill the remaining gap between the wall and the ceiling. These windows provide an airtight space, without hindering the entrance of light or the sensation of open space. Simple materials and found objects furnish the space and several of the building's original industrial components have now been put to domestic use. The artist restored and rewired old light fixtures left in the building's basement to light some part of the loft at night. Gauzy fabrics clipped to copper pipes were suspended from the ceiling to create 10-ft drapes that drift lazily in the breeze.

Cette usine textile reconvertie, située dans un ancien quartier industriel de Philadelphie, offre un mélange éclectique de styles, reflet de la personnalité et des goûts du propriétaire, artiste et directeur d'une galerie d'art à but non lucratif. Le studio du peintre est séparé de l'espace de vie par un mur de 2,5 m auquel le propriétaire a ajouté des fenêtres au châssis de bois ancien pour compléter l'espace entre le mur et le plafond. Grâce à ces fenêtres, l'espace est sec, lumineux et ouvert. Matériaux simples et objets chinés décorent l'espace. Plusieurs éléments, issus du bâtiment industriel d'origine, sont utilisés à des fins domestiques. L'artiste a restauré et rebranché certaines anciennes fixations de lampe trouvées au sous-sol du bâtiment pour éclairer certaines parties du loft, la nuit. Des tissus de tulle accrochés à des tuyaux de cuivre pendent du plafond pour créer des tentures de 3 m de long flottant dans l'air avec nonchalance.

Diese umgebaute Textilfabrik in einem alten Gewerbegebiet von Philadelphia bietet eine eklektische Mischung verschiedener Stilarten, welche die Persönlichkeit und den Geschmack ihres Besitzers widerspiegeln, einem Künstler und Direktor einer unabhängigen Kunstgalerie. Das Malstudio wird vom Wohnbereich durch eine 2,5 m dicke Wand getrennt, in die der Besitzer alte Holzfenster eingelassen hat, um die verbleibende Lücke zwischen Wand und Decke zu füllen. Der Raum ist mit einfachen Materialien und gefundenen Objekten ausgestattet und viele der ursprünglich gewerblich genutzten Komponenten wurden umfunktioniert. Der Künstler hat einige der alten Leuchten aus dem Keller renoviert und neu verkabelt, um einen Teil der Wohnung bei Nacht ausleuchten zu können. Hauchdünne Stoffe hängen an Kupferrohren von der Decke und bilden so ellenlange Vorhänge, die sanft im Wind schaukeln.

The space is furnished with simple materials and found objects. Several of the industrial components of the original building have been given domestic functions.

Matériaux simples et objets chinés meublent l'espace. Certains des éléments industriels de l'espace d'origine ont adopté aujourd'hui une fonction domestique.

Der Raum wurde mit einfachen Materialien und gefundenen Objekten dekoriert. Verschiedenen industriellen Komponenten des ursprünglichen Raumes wurde eine andere Funktion gegeben.

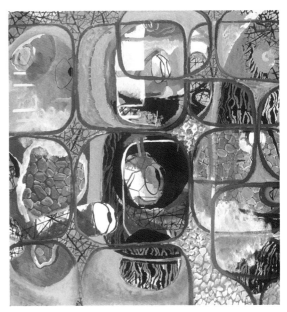

An eclectic mix of styles express the personality and tastes of its owner.

Un mélange éclectique de styles et d'objets, messagers de la personnalité et des goûts du propriétaire.

Eine eklektische Mischung an Stilrichtungen und Einzelteilen untersteichen die Persönlichkeit und den Geschmack des Besitzers.

Yudell-Beebe House
Maison Yudell-Beebe
Yudell-Beebe Haus

California, Unites States

This house was developed for a painter in close response to the rhythms and materials of the rugged coast of northern California. Movement through and around the house is choreographed to enhance the spatial and sensorial experience. The windows are designed to frame near and distant landscapes and revel in the plays of light. The courtyard, which faces northeast, catches the morning sun while also providing protection from the wind; the study towers, 16-ft high, also receive sunlight. The configuration of all the spaces ensures maximum exposures to the exterior, and thus optimal daylight and ventilation. The spaces are simply shaped but shift dramatically in height to present a layered sequence of framed views and paths.

Cette maison a été conçue pour un peintre, en étroite harmonie avec les rythmes et les matières du littoral découpé de la Californie du Nord. C'est une véritable chorégraphie du mouvement autour et dans la maison pour exalter l'expérience spatiale et sensorielle. Les fenêtres, à l'instar de tableaux, encadrent les vues proches ou lointaines du paysage et mettent en valeur les jeux de lumière. Le patio, face au nord-est, apprivoise le soleil matinal tout en protégeant du vent. Les tours qui abritent les ateliers, hautes de 4,5 m, sont aussi baignées de soleil. La configuration de tous les espaces maximalise l'exposition vers l'extérieur, pour une abondance de lumière du jour et une bonne ventilation. Les espaces aux formes simples s'élancent en hauteur créant une série d'encadrements de vues et de chemins.

Dieses Haus wurde für einen Künstler und Maler in Gedanken an den Rhythmus und das Material der rauen Küste Nordkaliforniens entwickelt. Das ganze Haus scheint in Bewegung zu sein und es ist innen und außen ein Gefühl von Raum und Sinneswahrnehmung zu spüren. Die Fenster bilden den Rahmen für verschiedene Landschaften und spielen mit dem Licht. Der nach Nordosten weisende Hof fängt das Morgenlicht ein und bietet gleichzeitig Schutz vor dem Wind. Die stabilen Türme werden ebenfalls von der Sonne umspielt. Die Konfiguration aller Räume sorgt für eine maximale Ausrichtung nach außen und daher optimale Ausnutzung des Tageslichts und der frischen Luft. Die Räume sind einfach gestaltet, unterscheiden sich aber extrem in der Höhe, um auf eine Sequenz gerahmter Ausblicke und Wege zu weisen.

This linear structure is laid out so that the interior spaces are exposed to the exterior at several points and receive plentiful sunlight and ventilation.

La structure linéaire est configurée de telle sorte que l'espace intérieur est constamment exposé vers l'extérieur recevant ainsi la lumière du jour en abondance et bénéficiant d'une aération optimale.

Die lineare Struktur wurde so konfiguriert, dass die Innenräume an verschiedenen Stellen nach außen orientiert sind und genügend Tageslicht einfällt.

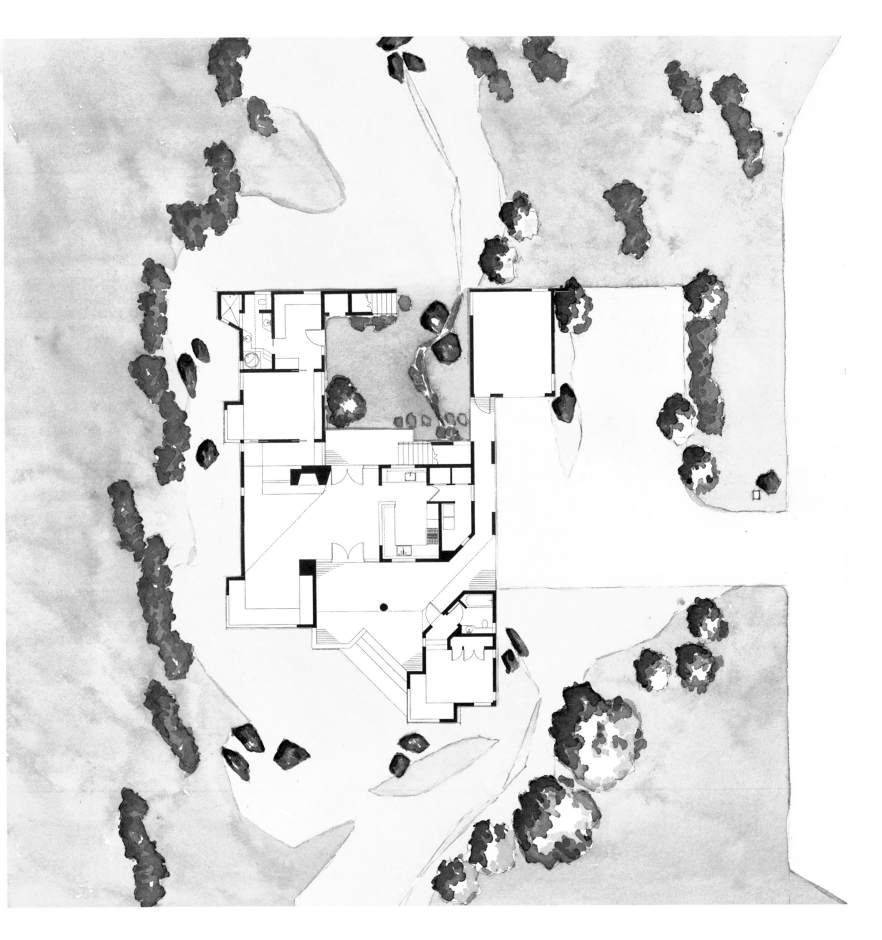

Loft in Paris
Loft à Paris
Loft in Paris

Paris, France

The design specialist who commissioned Christophe Pillet for this project decided to establish his work base in his own home. His Parisian loft was divided on two levels for the different activities taking place: the daytime areas, including the kitchen, dining room, toilet, study, and living room, were located downstairs. The bedroom, with its private bathroom, is upstairs. The architect tried to connect all the rooms visually to provide a sensation of spaciousness, and the vertical partitions that close off the bathroom and kitchen were fitted with a round glass window. Only one wall is external, so the main aim from the outset was to ensure that light could reach the home's innermost areas. The client's passion for art and designer furniture prompted the architect to choose floors and finishings in neutral colors, to create a warm setting in which decorative elements can stand out and take on a special role.

Le designer qui a engagé Christophe Pillet pour réaliser ce projet, a décidé de travailler chez lui. Son loft parisien s'articule donc sur deux niveaux en fonction des diverses activités qui s'y déroulent : en bas, les aires de jour, avec la cuisine, la salle à manger, les toilettes, le bureau et le salon, et en haut, la chambre à coucher avec sa salle de bains privée. L'architecte a essayé d'établir un lien visuel entre toutes les pièces pour accentuer la sensation d'espace. Une fenêtre ronde est insérée dans les cloisons verticales qui séparent la salle de bains et la cuisine. Il n'y a qu'un mur externe pour que la lumière puisse pénétrer partout jusqu'aux aires les plus intimes, objectif initial de la conception. Connaissant la passion pour l'art et les meubles design de son client, l'architecte a choisi de décliner les sols et les habillages en couleurs neutres, créant une ambiance chaleureuse où les éléments décoratifs ont un rôle particulier et y sont mis en valeur.

Der Designspezialist, der für dieses Projekt Christophe Pillet verpflichtete, wollte seinen Arbeitsplatz in das eigene Heim verlegen. Das Loft wurde in zwei Ebenen aufgeteilt, um Platz für verschiedene Aktivitäten zu bieten. Die Tagesbereiche wie Küche, Esszimmer, Toilette, Wohnzimmer sowie das Studio befinden sich unten. Das Schlafzimmer mit privatem Bad liegt oben. Der Architekt bemühte sich darum, alle Zimmer visuell miteinander zu verbinden, um ein Gefühl von Raum zu schaffen, und die vertikalen Verstrebungen, die Badezimmer und Küche abtrennen, sind mit einem runden Glasfenster versehen. Da eine Außenwand vorhanden war, galt es vorrangig, eine Möglichkeit zu schaffen, Tageslicht in die Innenbereiche eindringen zu lassen. Die Leidenschaft des Kunden für Kunst und Designermöbel haben den Architekten dazu angeregt, Böden und Wände in neutralen Farben zu halten, um eine warme Atmosphäre zu schaffen.

The client's passion for art and designer furniture required a neutral space in which functional and decorative elements stand out and take on a special role.

Passionné d'œuvres d'art et de mobilier design, le propriétaire a fait créer un espace neutre où éléments décoratifs et fonctionnels sont mis en valeur et jouent un rôle particulier.

Kunst und Designermöbel stehen hier inmitten eines neutralen Raumes, in dem die funktionellen und dekorativen Elemente eine besondere Rolle einnehmen.

Gaston Bertin
images de rien

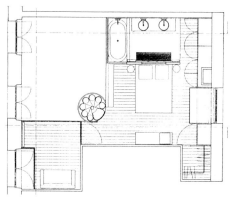

› First floor   Premier étage   Erstes Obergeschoss

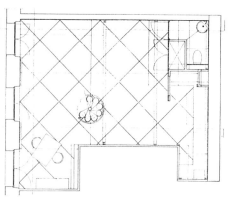

› Ground floor   Rez-de-chaussée   Erdgeschoss

Due to the limited size of the project, the architect designed connected spaces with openings in their walls that establish a visual relationship between them.

Limité par l'espace, l'architecte a conçu des pièces reliées entre elles par le biais d'ouvertures murales qui définissent la relation spatiale.

Der Architekt entwarf ein Konzept von Wänden, die mit Durchbrüchen versehenen sind, um eine visuelle Beziehung der einzelnen Räume zueinander zu unterstreichen.

Barcelona, Spain

Oriol Loft

The architect Oriol Roselló converted this old textile factory situated in Barcelona's Eixample district into a flat and studio/office for his own use. The rooms in the home open on to two patios, one of which is very spacious and becomes an improvised living area and dining room in hot weather. The office was divided into two areas, one on the side of the interior patio and the other in the loft situated next to the entrance. This upper level is distinguished by a mesh of metal beams supporting solid, wooden planks. It is reached by means of an unusual staircase divided into two parts: the first is an item of wooden furniture with shelves under the steps and the second is a metal module that hangs from the loft and leaves an empty space between the steps. The furniture in the apartment is an eclectic mix that combines designer pieces, such as Thonet's office chairs, with the other, humbler items in the kitchen.

L'architecte Oriol Roselló a converti cette ancienne usine textile du quartier Eixample de Barcelone, en un appartement et studio/bureau pour son usage personnel. Les pièces de la résidence s'ouvrent sur deux patios : lorsqu'il fait très chaud, le plus spacieux des deux se transforme en salon/salle à manger improvisés. Le bureau est divisé en deux zones, l'une sur le côté du patio intérieur, et l'autre dans le loft adjacent à l'entrée. Ce niveau supérieur est caractérisé par une ossature de poutres en métal qui soutiennent un robuste plancher. L'accès se fait par un escalier très original constitué de deux parties : la première est une composition murale en bois, garnie d'étagères, sous les marches et la deuxième est un module de métal suspendu au loft, laissant un vide entre les marches. Le mobilier de l'appartement est un mélange éclectique qui marie des œuvres de designer, à l'instar des chaises de bureau, à des objets plus ordinaires dans la cuisine.

Der Architekt Oriol Roselló hat diese alte Textilfabrik in Barcelona Eixample für sich selbst in einen Wohnraum und ein Studio verwandelt. Die Zimmer führen auf zwei Innenhöfe hinaus. Einer davon ist relativ groß und kann bei gutem Wetter als Wohn- und Essbereich genutzt werden. Das Büro ist in zwei Bereiche unterteilt: einen auf der Seite des Innenhofes und den anderen im Loft direkt neben dem Eingang. Die obere Ebene unterscheidet sich durch ein Netz von Metallbalken, das von soliden Holzplanken getragen ist. Man erreicht diese Ebene über eine ungewöhnliche Treppe, die zweigeteilt ist: Der erste Teil wird von einer Art Holzregal unter den Stufen gebildet, der zweite von einem Metallmodul, der vom Loft herunterhängt und einen leeren Raum zwischen den Stufen belässt. Die Möbel im Appartement bilden eine eklektische Mischung verschiedener Designerstücke wie z.B. ein Bürostuhl von Thonet.

The exterior areas increased the space available for the project and allow sunlight to flood into the interior.

Dans le projet, les espaces extérieurs accroissent la surface au sol utilisable et inondent l'intérieur de lumière naturelle.

Die äußeren Bereiche erweitern die Nutzbarkeit des Projektes und lassen natürliches Tageslicht ins Innere einfallen.

The furniture is eclectic but well matched, combining designer chairs like Thonet's office chairs with other simpler ones in the kitchen.

Le mobilier de l'appartement forme un ensemble éclectique car il associe des chaises design comme la chaise de bureau Thonet à d'autres meubles plus simples comme ceux de la cuisine.

Hier wurde ein eklektischer Mix an Möbeln zusammengestellt, darunter Thonet-Stühle, aber auch einfache Elemente im Küchenbereich.

Loft on Rue de Tunis
Loft de la rue de Tunis
Loft an der Rue de Tunis

Paris, France

This loft is the result of the refurbishment of a workshop in a thriving neighbourhood of the city. The project had to adapt to the form and openings determined by the different functions of the home, as well as articulating the overall layout and ensuring a sense of spaciousness. With this in mind, the great height of the workshop was exploited to open up a light-filled space on the top level, which houses the work area, kitchen and sitting room, while the ground floor is reserved for the bedrooms. The two levels are linked by a staircase clad in large sheets of exotic wood, which are also to be found in the bedrooms and in the expansive upper space, which receives sunlight through the side windows and the skylights in the roof. The warm atmosphere is the result of grouping elements with diverse influences in highly harmonious combinations.

Ce loft est le résultat de la restauration d'un atelier dans un quartier vivant de cette cité. Le projet devait tenir compte des formes et ouvertures déterminées par les différentes fonctions de la maison, redistribuer le plan de base et créer une sensation d'espace. Afin d'y parvenir, l'architecte a exploité l'immense hauteur de l'atelier pour agrandir l'espace très lumineux du niveau supérieur qui abrite l'aire de travail, la cuisine et le salon, alors que le rez-de-chaussée est réservé pour les chambres. Les deux niveaux sont reliés par un escalier constitué de grandes marches de bois exotique que l'on retrouve dans les chambres et dans l'immense étage supérieur inondé de lumière du soleil grâce aux fenêtres latérales et aux velux du toit. Des éléments regroupés en combinaisons harmonieuses, créent des effets divers et imprègnent l'espace d'une atmosphère chaleureuse.

Dieses Loft ist das Ergebnis der Neugestaltung eines Ateliers in einem beliebten Stadtviertel der Stadt. Das Projekt musste die Form und die Ausgänge an die verschiedenen Funktionen einer Wohnung anpassen und gleichzeitig den gesamten Grundriss auf ein Gefühl von Weite ausrichten. Die enorme Höhe des Ateliers wurde genutzt, um auf der oberen Ebene einen lichtdurchfluteten Raum zu schaffen, in dem Arbeitsbereich, Küche und Wohnzimmer untergebracht sind, während im Erdgeschoss die Schlafzimmer liegen. Die beiden Ebenen sind durch ein Treppenhaus aus Tropenholz miteinander verbunden, was auch in den Schlafzimmern und dem großen Raum oben eingesetzt wurde. Das warme Ambiente ist das Resultat der Gruppierung von Elementen mit verschiedenen Einflüssen in harmonischen Kombinationen.

The office is a small, bright room, equipped with a big bookshelf and a small desktop for a computer.

Le bureau est une petite pièce étroite lumineuse, équipée d'une grande étagère et d'un petit bureau pour ordinateur.

Das Büro ist ein kleiner, heller Raum mit einem großen Bücherregal und einem kleinen Computerschreibtisch.

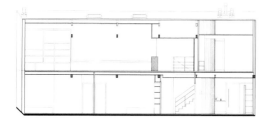

› Section Section Schnitt

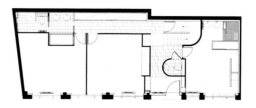

› Ground floor Rez-de-chaussée Erdgeschoss

› First floor Premier étage Erstes Obergeschoss

The open up a light-filled space on the top level locates the kitchen and sitting room.

La cuisine et le salon se trouvent au dernier étage, dans un espace ouvert et inondé de lumière.

In einem lichtdurchfluteten Raum auf der oberen Ebene sind Küche und Wohnzimmer untergebracht.

House in Northwoods
Maison à Northwoods
Haus in Northwoods

Minnesota, United States

The architect David Salmela was commissioned to enlarge a small cabin so that the owners could live in it for longer periods. The new building has three clearly differentiated sections: one of double height with a storeroom and bathroom; another two-story section with a living room below and guest room above; and a third, which has three levels for the main study, a computer area, and a loft at the top. The office level enjoys panoramic views of the exterior through the windows. Most of the interior is finished with cedar, although maple is used for the horizontal features and the flooring is slate. All the new structures have been stained black—the same color used to paint the cedar logs of the buildings already on the site. This camouflages the house with its surrounding environment.

L'architecte David Salmela a agrandi une petite cabane pour que son propriétaire puisse y séjourner plus longtemps. La nouvelle construction possède trois parties bien définies : l'une, à double hauteur, abrite un débarras et une salle de bains, l'autre est à deux étages avec en bas un salon et en haut une chambre d'amis. La dernière, à trois niveaux, accueille le bureau principal, la pièce d'ordinateur et le loft, tout en haut. Le bureau est doté de fenêtres offrant une vue panoramique sur l'extérieur. Presque tout l'intérieur est en cèdre. L'érable habille les éléments horizontaux et l'ardoise recouvre le sol. Toutes les nouvelles structures sont teintes en noir –couleur des rondins de cèdre des constructions préexistantes sur le site. Il s'en dégage une impression de camouflage de la maison dans le paysage environnant.

Der Architekt David Salmela wurde damit beauftragt, eine kleine Hütte zu vergrößern. Das neue Gebäude sollte drei klar voneinander abgetrennte Bereiche aufweisen: einen sehr hohen mit Lagerraum und Badezimmer, einen weiteren zweistöckigen Bereich mit einem Wohnzimmer unten und einem Gästezimmer oben, und einem dritten, der drei Ebenen für das Hauptatelier, einen Computerbereich und ein Loft darüber bietet. Von der Büroebene aus genießt man einen herrlichen Blick auf die Umgebung. Das Innere ist fast überall mit Zedernholz verkleidet, Ahorn wurde für horizontale Details verwendet und der Boden ist aus Schiefertafeln gelegt. Alle neuen Strukturen sind schwarz gefärbt wie die Zedernholzbalken, die man auf dem Grundstück gefunden hat. Dadurch fällt das Haus in dieser Umgebung fast gar nicht auf und fügt sich nahtlos in die Landschaft ein.

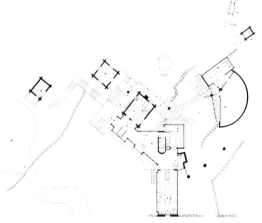

› Plans Plans Grundrisse

Studio in Manhattan
Studio à Manhattan
Studio in Manhattan

New York, United States

This 3,000-sq.-ft loft was designed to accommodate a residence and a professional recording studio for a composer. In the center of the loft stands a mahogany structure inspired by a Japanese bathhouse, including an open shower, concrete soaking tub, mahogany vanity, and changing room. The living area is based on the layout of an Islamic courtyard garden and incorporates a water element that serves as a welcoming and cleansing fixture near the entrance. The recording studio was conceived as a box within a box to achieve acoustic isolation. The room incorporates high-tech audiovisual equipment and acoustically insulated panels wrapped in silk fabrics. The electronic installations throughout the loft permit the owner to record music from any room, creating a completely integrated living/working environment.

Ce loft de 280 m² a été conçu pour devenir la résidence et le studio d'enregistrement professionnel d'un compositeur. Le centre du loft est occupé par une structure en acajou inspirée d'une salle de bains japonaise, avec une douche ouverte, une baignoire en béton, un plan de toilette en acajou et une pièce pour se changer. Le salon est conçu à l'instar d'un patio arabe avec un jardin et un point d'eau, accessoire de toilette et d'accueil, près de l'entrée. Le studio d'enregistrement est conçu comme une « boîte dans une boîte » pour garantir l'isolation acoustique. La pièce est dotée d'un équipement audiovisuel high-tech et de panneaux insonorisés, enveloppés de soie. Les installations électroniques permettent au propriétaire d'enregistrer de la musique dans toutes les pièces du loft, créant un environnement où travailler et vivre ne font qu'un.

Dieses 280 m² große Loft sollte einem Komponisten sowohl Wohnraum als auch ein professionelles Aufnahmestudio bieten. In der Mitte steht eine Mahagoni-Struktur, die einem japanischen Badehaus ähnelt. Darin befinden sich eine Dusche, eine Badewanne, ein Waschtisch aus Mahagoni und ein Ankleidezimmer. Der Wohnbereich basiert auf dem Layout eines islamischen Hofgartens und enthält ein Wasserspiel, das Gäste willkommen heißt und gleichzeitig die Raumluft reinigt. Das Aufnahmestudio wurde als Kasten in einem Kasten konzipiert, um die Akustik abzuschirmen. Das Zimmer bietet eine hochmoderne audiovisuelle Ausstattung und akustisch isolierte Trennwände, die mit Seide verkleidet sind. Die elektronische Installation im gesamten Loft erlaubt es dem Besitzer, die Musik von jedem der Zimmer aus aufzunehmen, weil Arbeits- und Wohnbereich hier wirklich nahtlos ineinander übergehen.

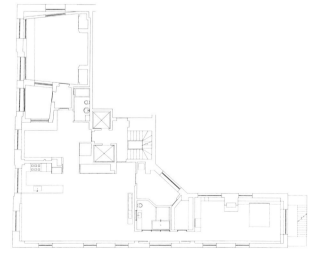

› Plan Plan Grundriss

Doctor's Practice
Cabinet médical
Arztpraxis

Paderborn, Germany

This one-story building contains the office of a doctor specializing in internal medicine, and is divided into nine sections measuring 270 sq. ft each. The main consulting room is lit by a skylight, which also illuminates the entrance and corridors. Panels open and close to control ventilation and to regulate the amount of sunlight entering inside. The interior strongly reflects the metal framework, which distributes weight by means of a wooden beam system. The house's layout is simple: rooms follow one another, varying in function, materials, light, and temperature. The façade is a continuous wall of reinforced concrete that provides visual and thermal isolation. Inside, along the wall, a passageway connects the different rooms and doubles as an art gallery. During the coldest months, the large windows are closed and it becomes a greenhouse, with a under-floor heating system.

Ce bâtiment d'un étage, divisé en neuf sections de 25 m² chacune, abrite le bureau d'un docteur spécialisé en médecine interne. La salle principale de consultation reçoit la lumière d'un velux qui éclaire aussi l'entrée et le couloir. Des panneaux s'ouvrent et se ferment pour régler la ventilation et la quantité de soleil pénétrant l'intérieur. Une structure en métal, dont le poids est réparti par un système de poutres de bois, caractérise l'intérieur. Le plan de la maison est simple : une enfilade de pièces, changeant de fonctions, de matériaux, de lumière et de température. La façade est un mur continu de béton armé, qui assure protections visuelle et thermique. A l'intérieur et le long du mur, un couloir relie les différentes pièces et fait aussi office de galerie d'art. Pendant les mois les plus froids, les grandes fenêtres sont fermées et le passage se métamorphose en serre dotée d'un système de chauffage au sol.

Dieses eingeschossige Gebäude bietet Raum für die Praxis eines Internisten und ist in neun Bereiche aufgeteilt, die jeweils 25 m² messen. Das Hauptbehandlungszimmer wird von einem Dachfenster ausgeleuchtet, dessen Licht auch in den Eingangsbereich und die Flure fällt. Die Belüftung und Beleuchtung wird durch bewegliche Paneele gesteuert. Innen ist ein metallenes Gerüst sichtbar, das das Gewicht über ein ausgeklügeltes System von Holzbalken verteilt. Der Grundriss ist einfach gehalten: Ein Zimmer folgt dem nächsten und variiert in Funktion, Material, Licht und Temperatur. Die Fassade ist eine kontinuierliche Mauer verstärkten Betons, der eine visuelle und thermische Isolierung gewährleistet. Im Inneren verbindet ein Flur die einzelnen Zimmer miteinander und dient gleichzeitig als Kunstgalerie. Während der kältesten Monate werden die großen Fenster geschlossen und bilden so einen Wintergarten mit Fußbodenheizung.

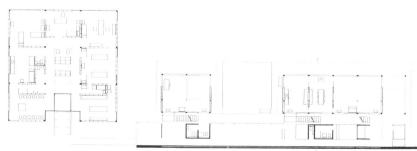

› Ground floor Rez-de-chaussée Erdgeschoss

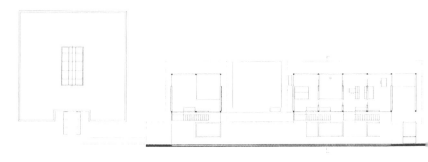

› First floor Premier étage Erstes Obergeschoss

The system of beams used to hold up the roof is visible on the terrace and serves as a reminder of the building's past.

Le système de poutres qui soutenait le toit est visible sur la terrasse, symbole de continuité avec le projet d'origine.

Das Balkensystem, mit dem das Dach getragen wird, ist auf der Terrasse sichtbar und erinnert an die Kontinuität des originellen Projektes.

Loft in Majorca
Loft à Majorque
Loft auf Mallorca

Majorca, Spain

The first step in the renovation project for this warehouse was the creation of large, discreetly framed glass panels to separate the building's entrance from the lobby and reveal glimpses of the impressive interior from outside. The large half-height partitions were employed to differentiate areas and emphasize the dimensions of the loft. A concrete staircase leads upstairs to a studio and meeting room, separated by sliding partitions. The pitched ceiling remains exposed throughout. Rugs were laid to supply a more personalized atmosphere. Another partition, flanked by two columns, divides the office and the kitchen. From here, one can appreciate the encompassing structure of the loft. A recent addition to the top floor includes the kitchen/dining areas, living room, and bedroom. The all-white bedroom establishes an attractive color contrast and a pure, light feel.

La rénovation de cet entrepôt a commencé par l'installation de grandes cloisons de verre insérées dans un châssis discret pour séparer l'entrée de l'édifice du lobby tout en permettant, de l'extérieur, d'apercevoir le magnifique intérieur. Les grandes cloisons à mi-hauteur, servent à différencier les zones et à exalter les dimensions du loft. Un escalier de béton dessert un studio et une salle de réunion, situés à l'étage et séparés par des cloisons coulissantes. Le plafond en pignon est apparent. Des tapis personnalisent l'atmosphère. Une autre cloison, flanquée de deux colonnes, sépare le bureau et la cuisine. De là, on peut admirer la magnifique structure du loft. Cuisine/salle à manger, salon et chambres à coucher ont été récemment installés à l'étage supérieur. Le blanc intégral de la chambre à coucher, marque un intéressant contraste de couleur et ajoute un sentiment de pureté et de légèreté.

Der erste Schritt dieses Renovierungsprojektes eines Lagerhauses war der Bau eines großen, diskret gerahmten Glaspaneels, um den Eingang des Gebäudes von der Lobby zu trennen und einzelne Blicke von außen auf das beeindruckende Innere zu ermöglichen. Eine große, halbhohe Wand trennt die einzelnen Bereiche voneinander ab. Eine Betontreppe führt nach oben zu einem Studio und einem Konferenzraum, die durch eine Schiebetür getrennt sind. Das aufgeschlagene Dach ist überall sichtbar. Teppiche sorgen für ein gemütliches Ambiente. Eine weitere Wand, die von zwei Säulen abgeschlossen wird, trennt Büro und Küche. Von hier aus kann man die herrliche Struktur des Lofts genau einsehen. Ein Anbau im oberen Stockwerk bietet Platz für Küche/Essraum, Wohnzimmer und Schlafzimmer. Das ganz in Weiß gehaltene Badezimmer bietet einen attraktiven Farbkontrast.

Large half-height partitions were employed to differentiate areas and to emphasize the dimensions of the loft.

De grandes cloisons à mi-hauteur servent à diviser l'espace et mettent en relief les dimensions du loft.

Große, halbhohe Trennwände grenzen die einzelnen Bereiche voneinander ab.

This warehouse preserves its industrial character in terms of both the exterior and the interior.

Cet entrepôt a conservé son caractère industriel à l'intérieur comme à l'extérieur.

Bei diesem Lagerhaus wurde der gewerbliche Charakter sowohl im Inneren als auch im Außenbereich bewahrt.

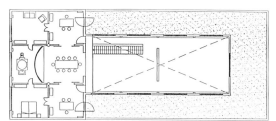

› First floor Premier étage Erstes Obergeschoss

› Ground floor Rez-de-chaussée Erdgeschoss

A concrete staircase leads upstairs to a studio and meeting room, separated by sliding partitions.

Un escalier en béton dessert le studio et la salle de conférence situés à l'étage, séparés par des cloisons coulissantes.

Eine Betontreppe führt nach oben zu einem Studio und Konferenzraum, die durch eine Schiebetür voneinander getrennt sind.

A recent addition to the top floor includes kitchen/dining areas, a living room, and a bedroom.

L'étage supérieur a été agrandi pour abriter une cuisine/salle à manger, un salon et une chambre à coucher.

Ein Anbau im oberen Stockwerk bietet Platz für Küche/Essraum, ein Wohnzimmer und ein Schlafzimmer.

A partition, flanked by two columns, divides the office and the living area.

Une cloison, flanquée de deux colonnes, sépare le bureau du salon.

Eine Trennwand, die von zwei Säulen eingerahmt wird, grenzt Büro und Küche voneinander ab.

The new living area is wrapped in metal siding and adorned with a bright red leather sofa.

La nouvelle salle de séjour est habillée d'un revêtement en métal et parée d'un divan de cuir rouge.

Der neue Wohnbereich ist mit Metall verkleidet worden. Besonders auffallend ist das hellrote Ledersofa.

The all-white bedroom creates an attractive color contrast and a light, heavenly feel.

La chambre à coucher, d'une blancheur totale, offre un contraste de couleur intéressant conjugué à une sensation de divine légèreté.

Das ganz in Weiß gehaltene Badezimmer bietet einen attraktiven Farbkontrast und wirkt elegant und freundlich zugleich.

House in Los Angeles
Maison à Los Angeles
Haus in Los Angeles

Los Angeles, United States

Extensive remodeling over the years has produced a viable living and working space that satisfies both the personal and professional needs of two architects. This house is reached by stairs that lead to a public entrance for guests and a back door for the family. Inside, a single staircase closed off from the living quarters leads from the ground floor to the third-floor office lobby. The building has a total surface area of about 6,000 sq. ft, with all the 2,000 square feet of the third floor occupied by the office.The third floor was gradually been modified through the addition of windows, skylights, built-in desks, bookshelves, and specialized areas designed for maximum effect and efficiency. Areas under the sloping gabled roof slopes too low for standing or walking were used for storage, desktops, and computer equipment. Models of old buildings line the ceiling to provide inspiration for future work.

Suite à une rénovation importante étalée sur plusieurs années, la construction s'est transformée en espace habitable, également adapté aux besoins professionnels de deux architectes. Des escaliers mènent à l'entrée officielle de cette maison : une porte à l'arrière est l'accès privé pour la famille. A l'intérieur, un seul escalier séparé des zones de vie part du rez-de-chaussée et conduit au troisième étage, réservé aux bureaux. La superficie totale au sol est de 550 m² environ y compris les 185 m² de bureaux occupant le troisième étage. Le troisième étage a été modifié peu à peu en ajoutant fenêtres, velux, bureaux intégrés, étagères et zones spécialisées pour un maximum d'efficacité et d'effet. Les espaces situés sous les pentes du pignon, trop bas pour y tenir debout, sont utilisés comme zones de rangement, bureaux et équipement informatique. Le plafond est recouvert de modèles d'anciens édifices, source d'inspirations pour de futurs projets.

Eine umfangreiche Neugestaltung im Laufe der Jahre schuf die Grundlage für einen Wohn- und Arbeitsbereich, der den persönlichen und beruflichen Anforderungen zweier Architekten gerecht wird. Dieses Haus in ist über eine Treppe erreichbar, die zu einem öffentlichen Eingang für Gäste und einer Hintertür für die Familie führt. Im Inneren führt eine einfache Treppe vom Erdgeschoss zur Bürolobby im 3. Stock. Das Gebäude umfasst 550 m², wobei die gesamten 185 m² der 3. Etage vom Büro belegt werden. Das Haus wurde zunächst nicht bewohnt und die 3. Etage wurde nach und nach durch den Einbau von Fenstern, Dachfenstern, Tischen, Regalen und funktionalen Bereichen verändert. Die Bereiche unter dem schrägen Giebeldach, die zum Stehen zu niedrig waren, wurden zu Lagerzwecken von Computern oder Zubehör genutzt. Modelle alter Gebäude verzieren die Decke, um Inspiration für zukünftige Arbeiten zu bieten.

Over the years, this floor was modified with the addition of windows, skylights, built-in desks, bookshelves, and specialized areas designed for maximum effect and efficiency.

Au fil des années, l'étage a été modifié en ajoutant fenêtres, velux, bureaux intégrés, étagères et des zones spécifiques conçues dans un souci d'efficacité extrême et d'effet maximum.

Im Laufe der Jahre wurde diese Etage mit Fenstern, Dachluken, eingebauten Tischen, Regalen und Bereichen versehen, die für maximalen Effekt und Effizienz sorgen.

Workshop in Belleville
Atelier à Belleville
Werkstatt in Belleville

Paris, France

A young photographer and her husband commissioned the architect François Muracciole to transform this old workshop at the end of a small patio. The idea was to take advantage of the elements that contributed to the space's original character and alluded to the workshop that was once located here. The patio, located in the center of the space, had been hidden by a plastic ceiling. Once this ceiling was removed, the sun could illuminate the entire space, including the bedrooms situated in the old warehouse. A large window overlooks the patio and there is also a loft that functions as a guest bedroom or TV room. When the patio is opened during the summer, the living room becomes an open-air space. All the objects and the details of the finishes help preserve the spirit of the former workshop.

Une jeune photographe et son mari ont engagé l'architecte François Muracciole pour restaurer cet ancien atelier situé au bout d'une petite cour. L'idée de base était de tirer parti des éléments imprimant à l'espace son caractère original, réminiscences de l'atelier d'autrefois. Le patio, au centre de l'espace, avait été fermé par un dôme en plastique. Sa suppression a permis de faire entrer le soleil et d'inonder l'espace de lumière y compris les chambres situées dans l'entrepôt. Une grande fenêtre surplombe le patio. La chambre d'amis et la salle de télévision sont situées dans un loft. En été, grâce au patio ouvert, le salon devient un espace à ciel ouvert. L'ensemble des objets et des détails de finition permet de préserver le cachet de l'ancien atelier.

Eine junge Fotografin und ihr Mann haben den Architekten François Muracciole beauftragt, diese alte Werkstatt am Ende eines kleinen Innenhofes umzubauen. Ziel war es, die Elemente mit einzubeziehen, die den Charakter dieses Raumes ausgemacht haben. Der Patio, der sich im Zentrum des Raums befindet, war mit einer Plastikdecke abgehängt. Sobald diese Decke entfernt war, konnte Tageslicht in den gesamten Raum einfallen, sogar in die Schlafzimmer, die sich im alten Lager befinden. Ein großes Fenster zeigt auf den Innenhof und ein Loft fungiert als Gästezimmer oder Fernsehraum. Im Sommer kann der Innenhof geöffnet werden und das Wohnzimmer befindet sich dann unter freiem Himmel. Alle Objekte und Details der Dekoration erinnern an das ehemalige Atelier.

The actual use of the space, as well as the decorative details, alludes to the original character of the mechanical workshop.

L'utilisation actuelle de l'espace et l'ensemble des objets et des détails de finition permettent de préserver le caractère original de l'ancien atelier mécanique.

Die aktuelle Nutzung des Raumes sowie die dekorativen Details spielen auf den ursprünglichen Charakter der Werkstatt an.

This apartment is a showcase of recycled space and furniture, whose charm suggests its former use.

Cet appartement est un exemple d'espace et de meubles recyclés dont le charme n'est pas sans rappeler sa fonction initiale.

Dieses Appartement ist ein Modell eines wiederverwerteten Raumes und ebensolcher Möbel, deren Charme an den vorherigen Nutzen erinnert.

Buecheler House
Maison Buecheler
Haus Buecheler

Berlin, Germany

This enormous old apartment, measuring 4,120 square feet, provides enough space for a home, workshop and art gallery, with 9 rooms that are fluidly interconnnected. The conversion respected the classic aristocratic style while introducing modern features. So, the original stucco roof, dating from 1904, was restored and the old parquet floors were sanded down and varnished. All rooms are characterized by white painted walls and large windows, enhancing the feeling of spaciousness and creating a bright, friendly atmosphere. The enormous built-in closet library serves as a separation wall between the living room and the art salon, and combined with other unique furniture pieces, forming a spirit of contradictions. The modern paintings and installations are the work of the residents Peter and Annette Buecheler, and they are put on show in the exhibitions regularly held in the apartment's very own art salon.

Cet énorme appartement, qui mesure 383 m², est suffisamment spacieux pour accueillir un atelier, une galerie d'art et neuf pièces qui communiquent entre elles. La restauration a respecté le style aristocratique classique tout en introduisant des éléments modernes. Le toit décoré de stucs, datant de 1904, a été entièrement restauré et l'ancien parquet poncé et vitrifié. Toutes les pièces présentent les mêmes caractéristiques : murs blancs et grandes fenêtres qui accentuent la sensation d'espace et créent une atmosphère gaie et conviviale. L'immense bibliothèque intégrée sert de mur de partition entre la salle de séjour et le salon d'art. Combinée à d'autres pièces d'ameublement uniques, elle forme un mélange riche en contrastes. Les peintures et installations modernes sont l'œuvre des habitants Peter et Annette Buecheler qui les exposent régulièrement dans leur salon d'art privé.

Dieses riesige alte Appartement, das sich über 383 m² erstreckt, bietet ausreichend Platz für eine Wohnung, ein Atelier und eine Galerie, insgesamt 9 Räume, die nahtlos ineinander übergehen. Bei der Renovierung wurde der klassische, aristokratische Stil beibehalten, gleichzeitig aber auch modernen Funktionen Raum geboten. Die original Stuckdecke aus dem Jahr 1904 wurde restauriert und der alte Parkettboden aufgearbeitet. Alle Zimmer wurden weiß gestrichen und zeichnen sich durch große Fenster aus, was die Weiträumigkeit unterstützt und eine helle, freundliche Atmosphäre schafft. Die riesige, eingebaute Schrankbibliothek dient als Trennwand zwischen Wohnzimmer und Kunstsalon, die gemeinsam mit ein paar einzigartigen Möbelstücken ein Ambiente der Gegensätze bilden. Die modernen Bilder und Installationen sind Arbeiten der Bewohner Peter und Annette Bucheler und werden regelmäßig im eigenen Kunstsalon vorgeführt.

The modern paintings and installations are the work of the residents Peter and Annette Buecheler.

Les peintures modernes et les installations sont l'œuvre des habitants Peter et Annette Buecheler.

Die modernen Bilder und Installationen sind Kunstwerke der Bewohner Peter und Annette Buecheler.

The kitchen is painted black and equipped with black and chrome furniture, creating an very elegant style.

La cuisine peinte en noir, équipée de meubles alliant le noir et le chrome, est très stylée.

Die Küche ist schwarz gestrichen und mit schwarzen Möbeln und Chromdetails ausgestattet, was ein ausgesprochen elegantes Ambiente schafft.

São Paulo, Brazil

Campana Loft

This project, supervised by the architect Fernando Campana, involved an expanse of 2,475 sq. ft in a commercial building from the 1940s set in a residential district in downtown; it created a studio, exhibition space, and residence. The building, made of concrete blocks, was originally divided into two parts in the front and rear of the plot, joined by common bathrooms. The upper story of the front section was converted into a large exhibition area and living space. The rear of the building became a workshop and kitchen. The lower floor was transformed into a bedroom with a bathroom, while the old toilets were demolished to make way for a magnificent open-air patio. It was decided to leave the concrete staircase untouched, in order to enhance the overall industrial feel. A large steel-framed window was installed in the back wall to take full advantage of the natural light and provide a view of the subtly landscaped patio.

Dirigé par l'architecte Fernando Campana, ce projet prévoit l'agrandissement d'un bâtiment commercial des années 40, situé dans un quartier résidentiel de la cité. Il comprend un studio, un espace d'exposition de 30 m² et une résidence. L'édifice en blocs de béton, est, à l'origine, divisé en deux parties, à l'avant et à l'arrière du terrain, réunies par des salles de bains communes. L'étage supérieur, côté façade, a été converti en vaste salle d'exposition et espace habitable. L'arrière du bâtiment abrite un atelier et une cuisine. L'étage inférieur accueille la chambre à coucher avec salle de bains, les anciennes toilettes ont été démolies pour faire place à un magnifique patio extérieur. L'escalier en béton préservé, rehausse le caractère industriel de l'ensemble. A l'arrière, une grande fenêtre dans un châssis d'acier, permet de bénéficier au maximum de la lumière naturelle et d'apercevoir le patio paysagér avec beaucoup de goût.

Dieses Projekt von Fernando Campana umfasst einen Raum in einem gewerblichen Gebäude aus den 40er Jahren in der Innenstadt. Hier sind ein Studio, eine Ausstellungsfläche und ein Wohnraum entstanden. Das Gebäude aus Betonziegeln war ursprünglich in einen vorderen und einen hinteren Teil aufgeteilt. Die obere Etage des Vorderbereichs wurde in eine große Ausstellungsfläche sowie Wohnraum verwandelt. Die Rückseite des Gebäudes wurde zu Atelier und Küche umgebaut. Die untere Etage beherbergt jetzt ein Schlafzimmer mit Bad, während die alten Toiletten einem wunderschönen Innenhof Platz gemacht haben. Es wurde entschieden, die Betontreppe beizubehalten, um den gewerblichen Charakter des Gebäudes zu unterstreichen. Ein großes Stahlfenster wurde in die hintere Wand eingelassen, damit das natürliche Tageslicht einfallen kann und gleichzeitig der Blick auf den liebevoll bepflanzten Innenhof ermöglich wird.

Various views of the project are shown: the façade of the building and the interior spaces, including the living room. The furniture was designed by the architect.

Différentes vues du projet : la façade du bâtiment et les espaces intérieurs, y compris le salon. L'architecte a créé lui même le mobilier.

Verschiedene Ansichten des Projektes: die Fassade und der Innenbereich mit Wohnzimmer. Der Architekt hat die Möbel selbst entworfen.

Alford Atelier

New York, United States

The painter and architect Elizabeth Alford needed a place where she could practice both of her professions, so she set out about creating a condensed, active, and dynamic workspace. The layout was designed in such a way that the living and working spaces are physically separated. This division is defined by both a long fluorescent tube that runs through them and the placement of furniture. A shelf unit, loaded with jars of the sand that the artist uses for her work, also divides the space visually. An industrial steel structure serves as an organizer and, at the same time, becomes a striking decorative element in its own right. The steel used for the organizer is repeated on the long desk and shelves in the office, while wood paneling is a common theme in both the ceilings and floors. Noble materials such as wood, along with the evocative color scheme, endow the space with exquisite warmth.

Elizabeth Alford, artiste peintre et architecte, avait besoin d'un endroit où exercer ses deux professions. Elle a donc conçu un espace de travail compact, motivant et dynamique prévoyant la séparation physique des espaces de vie et de travail au moyen d'un long tube fluorescent qui les traverse et de l'agencement du mobilier. Un système d'étagères chargées de pots contenant le sable nécessaire au travail de l'artiste permet aussi une division visuelle de l'espace. Une structure industrielle en acier organise l'espace et c'est aussi un formidable élément de décoration à part entière. L'acier utilisé pour cette structure se retrouve le long du bureau et des étagères. Les lambris sont récurrents sur les plafonds et les sols. La noblesse des matériaux, comme le bois, conjuguée à la combinaison évocatrice de couleurs confèrent à l'espace une ambiance chaleureuse des plus agréables.

Die Malerin und Architektin Elizabeth Alford wünschte sich einen Raum, in dem sie beiden Berufen nachgehen konnte. Sie entwarf also einen komprimierten, aktiven und dynamischen Arbeitsplatz. Der Grundriss wurde so gestaltet, dass Wohn- und Arbeitsbereiche voneinander getrennt bleiben. Die Trennung wird sowohl von einem langen, fluoreszierenden Rohr unterstrichen, das durch die Bereiche reicht, als auch durch die Art und Weise, wie die Möbel platziert sind. Eine Regaleinheit mit Gläsern voller Sand, den die Künstlerin für ihre Arbeit verwendet, unterteilt den Raum ebenfalls visuell. Eine industrielle Stahlstruktur dient als Regal und wird gleichzeitig zum dekorativen Element. Derselbe Stahl wurde auch für den langen Tisch und die Regale im Büro verwendet, während Decken und Böden mit Holz verkleidet sind. Edles Material wie Holz und eine sinnliche Farbgebung verleihen dem Raum eine exquisite Wärme.

A long fluorescent tube running along the ceiling and the placement of furniture define the division between living and working spaces.

Un long tube fluorescent qui court le long du plafond ainsi que l'emplacement du mobilier délimitent les espaces salon et travail.

Ein langes, fluoreszierendes Rohr führt an der Decke entlang. Gleichzeitig unterstreicht auch die Platzierung der Möbel die Trennung zwischen Arbeits- und Wohnbereich.

Noble materials, such as wood, and an evocative color scheme give the space an exquisite warmth.

Matériaux nobles, comme le bois, conjugués à une palette évocatrice de couleurs, imprègnent l'espace d'une chaleur tout en subtilité.

Edelmaterial wie Holz und eine sinnliche Farbgebung verleihen dem Raum eine exquisite Wärme.

The project, designed by Elizabeth Alford herself, pays as much attention to the interior decoration as the spatial qualities of the environment created.

Le projet conçu par Elizabeth Alford elle-même, met autant l'accent sur la décoration intérieure que sur les qualités spatiales de l'environnement créé.

Dieses Projekt wurde von Elizabeth Alford selbst entworfen und unterstreicht sowohl die Dekoration der Innenräume als auch die räumlichen Qualitäten der Umgebung.

House in Santa Cruz
Maison à Santa Cruz
Haus in Santa Cruz

Santa Cruz, Bolivia

The starting point for this project was the acquisition of an old metallic shed structure and concrete water tank that were salvaged by the architects at a demolition site. The layout embraces a home and studio, thereby allowing for the installation of independent spaces and adding an urban feel to a space unified underneath a continuous roof structure. The building is divided into two: the north-south axis incorporates the most interesting section of the roof, and so its view was left unobstructed by inserting a large skylight. The east-west axis is defined by the water tank and a central, open-air but dry patio. A pool and fountain reinforce the direction of this axis and form the central elements of the composition. The interior features high ceilings and well-lit spaces. Two impressive, solid Caoba wood pieces were used as tables in the dining room and studio.

L'acquisition d'une vieille cabane en métal et d'un réservoir d'eau en béton récupéré par les architectes sur un terrain de démolition sont à l'origine du projet. Le plan comprend un logement et un studio qui permet l'installation d'espaces indépendants et ajoute une touche urbaine à un espace unifié sous une immense toiture. Le bâtiment est divisé en deux : l'axe nord-sud intègre la partie la plus intéressante du toit, auquel on a inséré un immense velux. L'axe est-ouest se définit par le réservoir d'eau et un patio central à ciel ouvert. Cet axe est renforcé par une piscine et une fontaine qui forment les éléments clés de cet ensemble architectural. L'intérieur se caractérise par de hauts plafonds et des espaces lumineux. Deux impressionnants troncs massifs de caoba servent de tables dans la salle à manger et dans le studio.

Ausgangspunkt für das Projekt war der Erwerb eines alten Metallschuppens und eines Wassertanks aus Beton. Beides wurde von den Architekten aus einem Abbruchgelände geborgen. Der Grundriss weist eine Wohnung und ein Studio auf und ermöglichte so die Einrichtung voneinander unabhängiger Räume. Unter einer durchgängigen Dachstruktur wurde dem Raum ein städtischer Anstrich verliehen. Das Gebäude ist zweigeteilt: Die Nordsüd-Achse verfügt über den größten Bereich des Daches und wird durch ein großes Dachfenster erhellt. Die Ostwest-Achse wird vom Wassertank und einem zentralen Innenhof unter freiem Himmel definiert. Ein Pool und ein Springbrunnen verstärken die Ausrichtung dieser Achse und bilden die zentralen Elemente dieser Komposition. Im Inneren fallen die hohen Decken und die gut ausgeleuchteten Flächen auf. Zwei beeindruckende Holzstücke aus Caob wurden als Tische im Esszimmer und Studio verwendet.

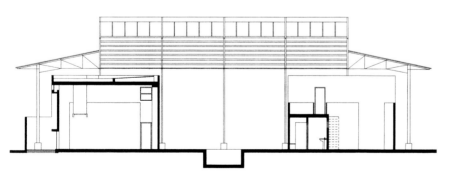

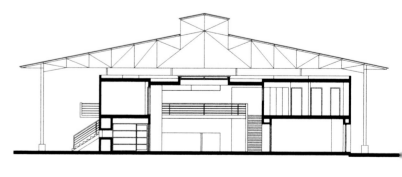

› Sections Sections Schnitte

Loft in Poblenou
Loft à Poblenou
Loft in Poblenou

Barcelona, Spain

The aim of this project was to achieve spaciousness and light, and the untouched structure offered more than 3,000 sq. ft of clear, open space. Massive windows occupy the perimeter of the loft, flooding the interior with natural light. A continuous resin pavement covers the floors, bouncing the light into every nook and cranny. The wooden floor on the upper level incorporates a series of glass inserts with built-in lamps that cast light upward. A staircase leads to the mezzanine level, which contains a den and an artist's workshop. The living and dining areas occupy the main space, which is dominated by a vast wall of windows. The decoration, developed by the designers and tenants, is minimalist and colorful, with certain modernist touches. The mixture of styles can be seen in the bathrooms, with one more minimalist and dominated by wood and translucent glass, the other more personalized, with a tile pattern imitated by the piles of books on the floor.

La structure existante, offrant plus de 280 m² d'espace ouvert et vide, a permis de créer un espace vaste et lumineux. D'immenses fenêtres sont installées tout autour du périmètre du loft, inondant l'intérieur de lumière naturelle. Un revêtement de résine homogène couvre les sols, renvoyant la lumière dans les moindres coins et recoins. A l'étage, des caissons de verre, avec éclairage intégré qui renvoie la lumière vers le haut, sont encastrés dans le plancher. Un escalier dessert la mezzanine, refuge et atelier de l'artiste. L'espace principal, doté d'un immense vitrage, abrite le salon et la salle à manger. La décoration, œuvre du designer et des propriétaires, est minimaliste, haute en couleurs et ponctuée de modernisme. Le mélange de styles définit les salles de bains : minimalisme et prédominance du bois et du verre translucide dans l'une, style plus personnalisé par le motif du carrelage à l'image des piles de livres sur le sol, dans l'autre.

Ziel dieses Projektes war es, ein Gefühl von Weite und Licht zu schaffen. Durch die massiven Fenster rund um das Loft dringt viel natürliches Tageslicht ein. Ein durchagängiger Belag aus Kunstharz bedecktden Boden und spiegelt das Licht wider. Der hölzerne Boden auf der oberen Ebene erhielt eine Reihe von Glaseinsätzen mit eingebauten Lampen, deren Licht nach oben scheint. Ein Treppenhaus führt in die Zwischenebene, in der ein Lagerraum und das Atelier liegen. Wohn- und Essbereich belegen den Hauptraum, der von einer großen Fensterwand dominiert wird. Die Dekoration, die von den Designern und Bewohnern entworfen wurde, ist minimalistisch und farbenfroh, geprägt durch moderne Details. Der Stilmix kann auch in den zwei Badezimmern bewundert werden, wobei das eine eher minimalistisch in Holz und Glas gehalten wird, das andere eine persönliche Note hat, mit Fliesenmustern, die einem Bücherhaufen auf dem Boden gleichen.

The decoration dreamed up by the designers and tenants is minimalist and colorful, with a few modernist touches.

La décoration, fruit de ses créateurs et des propriétaires, minimaliste et haute en couleurs est aussi empreinte d'une certaine touche de modernisme.

Die Dekoration, die von den Designern und Bewohnern entworfen wurde, ist eher minimalistisch und farbenfroh mit modernen Details.

The floors are covered with a continuous layer of resin that bounces the light up into every corner.

Un revêtement uniforme de résine couvre les sols, renvoyant la lumière dans les moindres coins et recoins.

Ein durchgängiger Boden aus Kunstharz spiegelt das Licht wider.

Dwelling on Rue Gobert

Maison de la rue Gobert

Haus in der Rue Gobert

Paris, France

The starting point for this loft for an artist was its setting of former cabinet-making workshops dating from the early 20th century, built around a narrow, rectangular courtyard. The project had to take advantage of the building's dimensions and two-directional orientation to create a versatile space that preserves the site's identity. A square volume was formed, with the functions structured around the alignment of four columns and a low, brightly colored partition in the dining room. In the main area, the kitchen is equipped with stainless-steel fittings. The dimensions of the sitting room allow it to fulfill several functions, including that of the studio in which the architect works. The only enclosed area is the private one, which also takes full advantage of the light; the design concept extends even to the closets, with their original wavy lines. The furniture provides splashes of color that contrast with the white walls and endow each setting with definition and structure.

L'origine de ce loft d'artiste est un ancien atelier d'ébénisterie datant du début du XXe siècle, construit autour d'un patio rectangulaire et étroit. Le projet devait tirer profit des dimensions de l'édifice et de deux orientations directionnelles pour créer un espace polyvalent tout en gardant l'identité du site. Le plan se présente sous forme de cube, alignant les fonctions le long de quatre colonnes et d'une cloison basse, haute en couleurs, dans la salle à manger. Dans la zone principale, la cuisine est équipée d'accessoires en inox. Grâce à ses dimensions, le salon peut avoir diverses fonctions dont celle d'un studio où l'architecte peut travailler. La sphère privée est la seule à être fermée mais bénéficie aussi de la lumière. Les commodes sont aussi très design avec leurs lignes courbes en forme de vague. Les armaires sont autant de touches de couleurs qui contrastent avec la blancheur des murs et qui caractérisent chaque pièce qu'ils structurent.

Dieses Künstlerloft wurde in einer ehemaligen Schrankwerkstatt aus dem frühen 20. Jh. untergebracht, die um einen engen, rechteckigen Hof herum gebaut wurde. Dabei sind die Ausmaße des Gebäudes und die zweidimensionale Ausrichtung mit einbezogen, um einen vielseitigen Raum zu schaffen. Die einzelnen Funktionen wurden um die Ausrichtung von vier Säulen und eine niedrige, grell bemalte Trennwand im Esszimmer herum angeordnet. Im Hauptbereich ist die Küche mit Edelstahlmöbeln eingerichtet. Die Dimensionen des Wohnzimmers erfüllen mehrere Funktionen gleichzeitig, darunter auch die des Studios, in dem der Architekt seiner Arbeit nachgeht. Der einzig in sich geschlossene Bereich ist der Privatbereich, der ebenfalls das Tageslicht voll nutzt. Das Designkonzept wurde sogar bis auf die Schränke mit ihren ursprünglichen Wellenlinien durchdacht. Die Möbel bieten Farbtupfer, die mit den weißen Wänden kontrastieren.

The sunlight entering through the windows on the southern face falls directly on to the sitting room and the studio.

Les rayons de soleil traversent les fenêtres de la façade sud pour inonder de lumière le salon et le studio.

Durch das Fenster im Süden fällt Tageslicht direkt in das Wohnzimmer und das Studio ein.

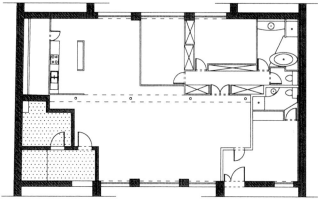

› Plan Plan Grundriss

Triple Function
Triple fonction
Dreifachfunktion

New York, United States

The clients in this project, a painter and her husband, who is an inventor and computer scientist, demanded three distinct types of spaces: private/domestic, public/studio, and private/studio. The architect opted for steel to provide a neutral yet rich backdrop for the artist's work as well as a futuristic and modern setting appropriate for the husband's work. The northernmost line segregates the private area of the loft, which contains the master bedroom and the bathrooms, while the southernmost line marks off the private studio, which includes the pottery workshop and meditation space. The remaining area of the apartment, between these two curved walls, comprises a kitchen and a painting studio. This open space is occasionally used as a gallery for public viewing sessions. In order to attain spatial fluidity and efficiency, a hinging system was designed along the walls so that nearly all the panels pivot as conventional closet or pantry doors.

A la requête des clients, une peintre et son mari, inventeur et informaticien, le projet traite trois différents types d'espace : privé/familial, studio/public et studio/privé. L'architecte a opté pour l'acier, toile de fond neutre mais luxueuse pour le travail de l'artiste et en même temps décor futuriste et moderne adapté au travail du mari. La sphère privée du loft, accueillant la chambre à coucher principale et les salles de bains, est située au nord. Le studio privé, situé au sud, héberge l'atelier de poterie et la salle de méditation. Le reste de l'appartement, inséré entre ces deux murs incurvés, accueille la cuisine et le studio du peintre. Cet espace ouvert, fait régulièrement office de galerie pour des expositions publiques. Pour plus de fluidité spatiale et d'efficacité, un système pivotant a été conçu le long des murs pour permettre aux panneaux de s'ouvrir comme des armoires traditionnelles ou des portes de placard.

Die Kunden, eine Malerin und ihr Mann, ein Erfinder und Computerwissenschaftler, baten um drei verschiedene Bereiche: privat/Haushalt, öffentlich/Studio und privat/Studio. Der Architekt entschied sich für Stahl, um einen neutralen, aber reichhaltigen Hintergrund für die Arbeit der Künstlerin zu bieten, aber auch, um der Arbeit des Ehemannes ein futuristisches und modernes Ambiente zu verleihen. Die nördliche Abgrenzung trennt den privaten Bereich mit Hauptschlafzimmer und Badezimmern, die südliche Abgrenzung trennt das private Studio, in dem ein Töpferatelier und Meditationsraum eingerichtet sind. Der verbleibende Bereich des Appartements zwischen den beiden gewölbten Wänden bietet Platz für die Küche und ein Malstudio. Der offene Raum wird gelegentlich als Ausstellungsraum genutzt. Entlang der Wände ist eine Hängevorrichtung angebracht, so dass fast alle Trennwände als konventionelle Schrankwand oder als Türen der Vorratskammer drehbar sind.

The open space intermittently serves as a gallery for public viewing sessions.

A certaines périodes de l'année, l'espace ouvert se transforme en galerie d'art accessible au public.

Der offene Raum dient mehrmals im Jahr als Galerie, in der die neuesten Werke vorgestellt werden.

In order to attain spatial fluidity and efficiency, a hinging system was designed along the walls so that nearly all the panels pivot like conventional closet doors.

Pour plus d'efficacité et de fluidité spatiale, un système pivotant a été conçu le long des murs pour permettre aux panneaux de s'ouvrir comme des armoires traditionnelles ou des portes de placard.

Entlang der Wände ist eine Hängevorrichtung angebracht, sodass fast alle Trennwände und konventionelle Schrankwände drehbar sind.

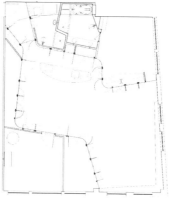

› Plan Plan Grundriss

The walls are made with laser-cut steel and punctuated by perforations created with state-of-the-art technology.

Les murs sont en acier coupé au laser et ponctué de perforations équipées d'une technologie de pointe.

Die Wände sind aus Stahl gefertigt und werden durch Perforationen unterbrochen, die mit hochmoderner Technologie angebracht werden konnten.

Alonso Planas House
Maison Alonso Planas
Alonso Planas Haus

Esplugues de Llobregat, Spain

This house lies on an elongated trapezoidal plot of land overlooking two valleys, with an entrance on a lower level, some fifty feet down from the mountain ridge. The layout was determined by the decision to place the main part of the residence on the upper section of the sloping land, producing level ground on both sides of the building to allow clear views across the valleys, to the south. The building has a basement dug into the mountain, and this is where the entrance, garage, and living space are located. The space created by the building's extended shape has been used to good advantage to create painting and sculpture workshops. Sunlight streams in through a large horizontal opening defined by a concrete and glass piece that provides a view of the upper patio. No partitions interrupt the space, leaving it open and flexible. The windows and doors were specially made, in white, in order to enhance the sense of light and breeziness.

La maison se situe sur un terrain trapézoïdal tout en longueur surplombant deux vallées, dont l'entrée est située en contrebas, environ 15 m en dessous de la crête de la montagne. La conception correspond à l'idée de placer la partie principale de la résidence en haut de la pente, permettant aux deux côtés de la maison d'être au niveau du sol et d'avoir une vue dégagée sur les deux vallées, vers le sud. Le sous-sol est creusé dans la montagne et abrite l'entrée, le garage et l'espace de vie. La forme allongée de l'édifice a permis de créer des ateliers de peinture et de sculpture. La lumière du soleil pénètre à flots par une grande ouverture horizontale alliant béton et verre et s'ouvrant sur le patio supérieur. L'espace, ouvert et flexible, n'est entravé par aucune cloison. Les fenêtres et portes sont spécialement réalisées en blanc pour exalter la sensation de lumière et de légèreté.

Dieses Haus steht auf einem trapezförmigen Stück Land und bietet einen herrlichen Blick auf gleich zwei Täler. Etwa 15 m unterhalb des Berghanges befindet sich der Eingang zum Haus. Der Grundriss wurde so ausgelegt, dass der Hauptteil des Gebäudes auf dem oberen Teil des abschüssigen Geländes liegt, sodass beide Seiten des Hauses auf ebenem Boden stehen. Ein Keller wurde direkt in den Berg gebaut, hier sind Eingang, Garage und Wohnbereich untergebracht. Der Raum, der durch diese Erweiterung frei geworden ist, wird heute als Mal- und Bildhaueratelier genutzt. Das Sonnenlicht fällt durch das große horizontale Fenster aus Beton und Glas ein, das auf den oberen Innenhof weist. Der Raum ist nicht unterteilt, sondern offen und flexibel. Fenster und Türen sind in Weiß gehalten, um den Eindruck von Licht und Frische zu verstärken.

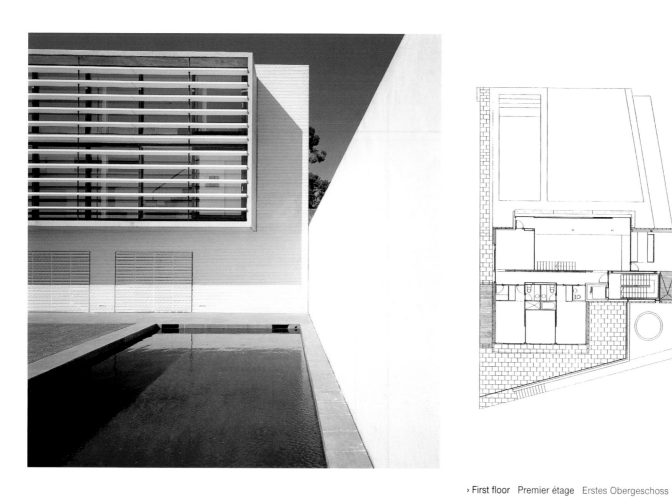

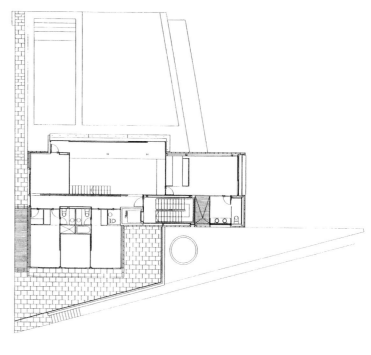

› First floor Premier étage Erstes Obergeschoss

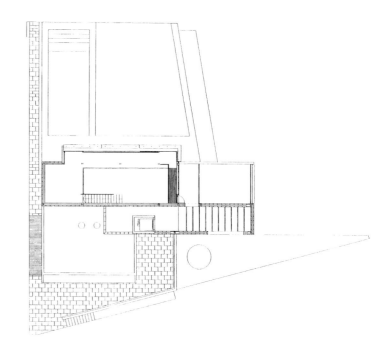

› Second floor Deuxième étage Zweits Obergeschoss

› Ground floor Rez-de-chaussée Erdgeschoss

378

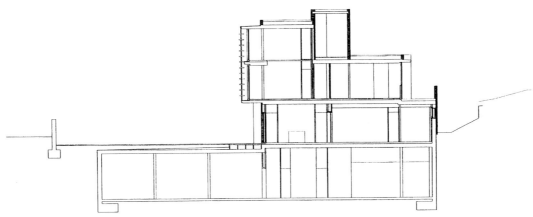

› Section Section Schnitt

The workshop, partially below ground, is illuminated by large, high windows. This long strip of glass provides constant ethereal light, ideal for painting.

L'atelier, en partie construit au sous-sol, est éclairé par de grandes fenêtres tout en hauteur. La grande bande de vitrage donne une lumière éthérée constante, idéale pour peindre.

Das Atelier liegt zum Teil unter der Erde und wird durch große, hohe Fenster beleuchtet. Das sorgt für ein ätherisches Licht, das sich ideal zum Malen eignet.

Photo Credits   Crédits photographiques   Fotonachweis